JIM CARREY

THE

CARREY

Joker is Wild

Martin Knelman

FIREFLY BOOKS

A FIREFLY BOOK

Published by Firefly Books Ltd. 2000

First Printing

U.S. CATALOGUING IN PUBLICATION DATA
Knelman, Martin
   Jim Carrey : The joker is wild/Martin Knelman.—
1st ed. [230] p. : col. ill. ; cm.
Originally published as : The joker is wild : the triumphs and tribulations of Jim Carrey. Canada : Penguin Group, 1999.
Includes index.
ISBN 1-55209-535-5
1. Carrey, Jim, 1962– . 2. Comedians–United States.
3. Motion picture actors and actresses – United States – Biography. I. Title.
791.43/028/092 [B]–dc21   2000   CIP

First published in the United States in 2000 by
Firefly Books (U.S.) Inc.
P.O. Box 1338, Ellicott Station
Buffalo, New York 14205

Printed and bound in Canada by
Friesens, Altona, Manitoba

for my fellow travelers
on the Lucca expedition:
Daniel Weinzweig, Beverley Slopen
and Bernadette Sulgit

CONTENTS

o o o o o o o

iNTRODUCTION

o o o o o o o o

WHEN HE was a schoolboy in Burlington, Ontario, the other kids counted on Jim Carrey's boisterous shenanigans to provide a break from classroom routine. Many years later, after a dizzying series of career advances, setbacks, comebacks and breakthroughs, it's still childlike goofiness that defines Carrey's special appeal. Carrey is a daredevil; he takes huge, risky leaps in both the physical and the creative sense. Even after becoming one of the world's biggest movie stars, he has retained a childlike eagerness to astonish the audience. He's always trying to confound our expectations, to make us gasp. Carrey gets high from playing without a net, and his ecstasy is contagious.

Carrey's career has been built on much more than juvenile behavior. It began with instinct and talent, which he honed single-mindedly for years. But if Carrey's success is the result of craftsmanship and hard work, there's something else that helps explain his bond with the audience. It's the fierce hunger that comes from a desperate past.

Throughout his surprisingly varied career—first as a singing impressionist on the stand-up comedy circuit, later as a brilliant satirist on the sketch-comedy TV series *In Living Color*, and more recently as the star of phenomenally popular movies—Carrey's unrestrained, hyperactive style of comedy has spoken to those of us who have never stopped craving disruptions and distractions. At his uninhibited best, he brings out the kid in everyone, defying all demands for responsible, adult behavior and leaving audiences in a state of liberated delirium.

Many other contemporary comedians have been successful doing childish routines, but no one taps our experience of childhood as richly and deeply as Carrey. It helps that approaching middle age he still has the physical charm and energy of an overgrown kid. His six-foot-two frame isn't quite as skinny as it used to be, but his body is still a wind-up toy capable of delightful contortions, as if he were made of Silly Putty. And when Carrey flashes his boyish grin, his teeth take on a life of their own, like one of the effects in a Victorian pop-up book.

No wonder it was six-year-olds who made *Ace Ventura, Pet Detective* a surprise hit. In *The Mask*, Carrey's genius for childish fantasy reached a peak when he became a whirling, manic, live-action cartoon character. And in *Dumb and Dumber* his portrayal of a well-meaning moron was touching as well as funny because he was able to suggest a vulnerable child in a grown man's body. Carrey was turning infantile regression into an art form.

Still, Carrey is by nature restless, and he has never been content to repeat himself. It was Woody Allen who remarked that as long as you're doing comedy you're sitting at the children's table, and in *The Truman Show* Carrey seemed to be trying to change the seating plan. Yet even in this restrained, self-consciously serious movie, Carrey gave the material some emotional power by making the oppressed hero seem like a lonely child surrounded by insensitive adults incapable of satisfying his needs.

For my money, Jim Carrey is the greatest comedian of his era. You have to go all the way back to the great silent clowns, Buster Keaton and Charles Chaplin, to find his peers in physical comedy.

There's a transcendent, celebratory quality about the way his gangly, goofily contorted frame bounces around in defiance of natural law. Yet Jim Carrey is anything but silent. His amazing gift for parody and lampoon—capable of interrupting a movie at any moment, like a burst of random channel-hopping—links some of his current movies to his early days as a singing impressionist. And Carrey combines the manic energy of a cartoon creature with the surest instinct for inspired mayhem since the Marx Brothers. The plots of his movies are often forgettable; their function is to provide an excuse to let Carrey run wild. And when he does, it's a holiday for the audience.

Still, I know people whose facial muscles tighten at the mere mention of Jim Carrey's name. They're quietly horrified that any educated person could actually enjoy the infantile shenanigans they associate with Carrey. To elitist snobs who recoil from slapstick stunts and bathroom humor, Carrey symbolizes the dumbing down of popular culture.

I don't share this attitude or have much sympathy for it, but I think I understand where it's coming from. A lot of educated moviegoers don't feel free to enjoy something unless it has certified respectability—and Jim Carrey doesn't have any intellectual or academic credentials. He's a grade nine dropout with no evident interest in world affairs or the arts. He has never been a social critic or even a satirist. Instead he's a miraculous reincarnation of a more traditional figure—the kind of great clown whose appeal crosses the usual dividing lines of social class and education.

Though Carrey may not be a deep thinker, he does have an intriguing dark side, with flashes of perversity and rage, which emerged in some of the sketches he did on TV and in his most daring departure from mainstream movies, *The Cable Guy*. This side of Carrey's talent gets an excuse to come out in *Man on the Moon* as he transforms himself into Andy Kaufman. In many ways Kaufman —a Jewish oddball from Long Island, New York—was the opposite of Carrey. The role takes Carrey into shadowy corridors he has never gone down before, and it gives him the kind of challenge that he now probably craves above all else. Yet when the performance is over, Jim Carrey returns to being who he is—which is infinitely more accessible, more versatile, more likable and more popular than Andy Kaufman ever was or could be.

Exploring the life of Jim Carrey, I found it impossible not to be affected by the poignant details of a childhood marked by family crises. The story of his formative years has no doubt had the effect of a private movie constantly replayed in his head for decades, and it's his response to those circumstances, along with his phenomenal talent, that has catapulted Jim to stardom.

Comedy was Jim Carrey's only way out. It was the one thing a frightened little boy learned to do that offered hope and escape. Carrey's dramatic life story is filled with echoes of the great childhood myths—*Peter Pan*, *Alice in Wonderland*, *The Wizard of Oz*, *Great Expectations*—but he has put his own spin on them and emerged as the hero. By making people laugh, he became a fixer. As a teenager, he was desperate for success, because it provided an alternative to anger and failure, and because, within the Carrey family, belief in Jim's talent had become a form of religion; his ascent to stardom represented a myth of the idealized afterlife that would cancel the pain.

Kelly Moran, who knew Carrey in his days at the Comedy Store in Los Angeles in the mid-1980s, recognized the frightened child in Jim Carrey who was using humor as a way to fend off scary demons. Carrey's ability to tap into the feelings associated with his own personal history might explain why millions of fans feel a strong connection with him.

The secret of Jim Carrey's phenomenal achievement may be that he has never lost his connection with the magic power he discovered when he was very young, which gave him the saving grace of feeling special. Years later, he's still inviting other kids into his funhouse and taking them on a wild ride. By staying true to the yearnings, suffering and escape routes of his own childhood, he has made it possible for some of us in the audience to reconnect with a part of ourselves we thought we had put behind us a long, long time ago.

hOOKED

PERCY CARREY would have loved spending Oscar night with Jim. Riding in the limo, strutting with that trademark italic gait of his, dropping cigarette ashes on the sleeve of his rented tuxedo, he would have been cracking jokes all the way, chortling at his own zingers. Many years earlier Percy had given up his dream of being a musician for the sake of a steady paycheck to support his wife and four children. But he had never given up his faith in the magic of show business, and his greatest dream became that one day his youngest child would achieve the kind of stardom that all Hollywood would applaud.

If he hadn't died in 1994 at the age of 67, there's no way Percy would have missed this big night. He would have been beaming with paternal delight, hobnobbing with Jim's celebrity friends and saying things like "That's my boy" and "Call me Perce" and "He's not just a ham, you know, he's the whole pig." And everybody who met Percy would say now they understood how Jim grew up to be so funny.

March 21, 1999, was the night of the last Academy Award rituals of the twentieth century, and much to the annoyance of his fans, Jim was not attending as a nominee. That was a much-talked-about snub, considering that two months earlier Carrey had won the Golden Globe award for best actor of 1998 in a dramatic movie for his subdued, no-kidding work in *The Truman Show*. Within a few years, he had made an amazing transformation. After *The Truman Show*, Jim was no longer regarded as a buffoon, known for talking out of his ass. He was emerging as a serious actor who could be placed on the same shortlist as Nick Nolte, Tom Hanks and Ian McKellen—and come out the winner.

Picking up his Golden Globe, Carrey not only thanked his parents (without mentioning both were dead), he also thanked the "members of the Academy." Then, drawing the biggest laugh of the night, he interrupted himself and explained: "I must have been thinking of something else."

That laugh turned a bit sour when the Academy announced its best actor nominees, and all four men Carrey had beaten in the Golden Globe race were on the list while his name was conspicuously missing. But instead of sulking, Jim accepted an invitation from the Academy to present the Oscar for best film editing. And on Oscar night, with his lanky, six-foot-two frame draped in a stylish all-black tuxedo ensemble designed by Donna Karan, Jim Carrey came out to present the award, flashed his winning, toothy smile—and began delivering a mock-poignant monologue about not being nominated.

"I'm here tonight to present the Academy Award for outstanding achievement in film editing," he announced, batting his big brown eyes with mock-sincerity. There was an ominous pause before he continued. "That's all I'm here to do." (Another pause.)

"I have nothing else to worry about. I can just...show up and enjoy the parties."

After an exaggerated, fake-happy sigh, Jim appeared to break down crying. Then came his faux-recovery line: "Winning the Oscar is not the most important thing in the world. It's an honor just to be nom...Oh, God!" At this point he feigned a complete breakdown and started bawling.

It was not only one of the few genuinely funny bits in a long, dreary evening, it was also a stunning illustration of how shrewdly and smoothly Jim Carrey manages his career. In a five-minute appearance, he had turned the subject of his own humiliation into a polished comedy sketch—and come out of it looking like a good sport. Besides being an accomplished comedian and actor, he had become a masterful spin doctor.

O   O   O

THOUGH HIS tears were fake that night, there had been many nights along the way when the tears that flowed were genuine. No matter how famous, rich and powerful he became, Jim could never quite shake frightening reminders of the bumpy ride he had endured. One of the most traumatic memories for both Jim and Percy was a night twenty-three years earlier in a grotty basement room on Church Street in downtown Toronto when Jim made his debut at Toronto's first comedy club, Yuk-Yuk's Komedy Kabaret.

In those days, not even the club's founder, Mark Breslin, thought of comedy as a viable business. Yuk-Yuk's, renting a long narrow room from a community center, was open just one night a week. The audience sat on benches. The small stage was adorned with a stool, two microphones and two floodlights. Dominating the room was a grotesque painting of two giant red lips. Every week there was one featured act, who got paid, and ten other unpaid performers—a mix of semi-pros and "kitchen table comics," cutups who had been breaking up the family at home and were encouraged by friends and relatives who said they belonged on stage.

In a way, Jim Carrey had been getting ready his whole life for this night. Yet if you were looking for a word to describe how he came across, the word would have to be "unprepared." He was a skinny, squeaky-voiced fourteen-year-old schoolboy (in grade nine) who had been entertaining his family and schoolmates for years with his gift for comedy and high-spirited mimicry. A lot of people said Jim got his zest for performing from his dad.

When Percy heard about Toronto's first comedy club, the news connected with his most cherished fantasies. In Percy's own mind he was a natural-born performer, and so was Jim—the only one of his four children with the talent and drive to reach the goal that had eluded Percy. What attracted Percy Carrey most was the fact that Yuk-Yuk's encouraged amateurs and wannabes. The new comedy club was, above all, democratic—pretty well anyone who showed up would get a chance to go on.

Almost everyone in the room that night was under the age of twenty-five, so Percy Carrey, with his thinning gray hair and rumpled suit, looked like someone's grandfather who had taken a wrong turn. Some people thought it was weird that a man of almost fifty, a conventional Catholic father from the boondocks, would bring his own teenage son to a place like Yuk-Yuk's. Percy seemed painfully out of place amid this crowd of the urban young and restless.

Nor was Percy there merely as an onlooker. He too had worked up an act, and he went on stage to deliver it before it was

Jim's turn. According to Joel Axler, Breslin's partner at the time, Percy Carrey didn't exactly have a stand-up monologue. Instead he told a string of semi-blue jokes. He was a bit like Archie Rice, the ferociously unfunny music-hall performer played by Laurence Olivier in John Osborne's *The Entertainer*. Percy's act might not have been great, but he was able to finish it and get off the stage without taking too much abuse from the crowd.

Jim was less fortunate. He came across as a goofy-looking, gangling kid who was so nervous he was almost jumping off the walls. Percy had managed to talk Jim into going on stage that night, but, lacking the instincts of a professional manager, he had failed to prepare Jim for the fact that this crowd would be totally different from the audiences Jim had captivated at school assemblies and family parties.

The kid was vulnerable and exposed. These people weren't in a mood to be warm and forgiving. It hadn't occurred to Jim that his function on this occasion was to be offered up as food for the sharks. His script had been written for him by Percy, and it wasn't tailored to this audience. Jim tried a few impressions, and they didn't go over. At one point he pulled his shirt over his knees and said, "Look, it's Dolly Parton!"

When it became apparent that his material wasn't working, Jim looked desperate. He began wildly goofing around and became even sillier—which made it all the more obvious that he had no material to fall back on. The kid looked like a scared deer caught in the headlights of an approaching car. There was only one thing to do: it was time to get the hook.

Mark Breslin had shrewdly decided that while bad acts could be tolerated, there had to be a way to make the ritual of acknowledging their badness fun for the audience. "We addressed the problem by developing cruel ways of removing people," Breslin explains.

The idea was to get an act that was bombing off the stage, but in an entertaining way. That's where the hook came in. It was made of a cut-off broomstick attached to a cardboard scythe covered in tinfoil. Joel Axler was in charge of operating the hook. Axler's methodology was basic: "I'd get the hook around the guy's waist and give it a good pull."

While Axler snared Jim Carrey with the notorious hook, the audience heard a tape-recording featuring the screeching voice of Mark Breslin: "It's a *dis-as-ter*," Breslin exclaimed, stretching out the syllables. Then there was a pause followed by the sound of a car crash and finally Breslin's voice saying: "Yes, it's another Yuk-Yuk's disaster!"

For the fourteen-year-old novice this was indeed a disaster—a traumatic and humiliating night to remember. It was one of the rare occasions when Jim Carrey was incapable of getting a laugh.

What no one in the crowd realized was that Jim wasn't just an inexperienced kid making funny faces. The Carrey family were staring into an abyss, and Jim's talent was about the only resource they had left. That night, he had been trying to come to the family's rescue. Instead they had to drive home in the dark with their fantasies shattered. And before the first of Jim's many comebacks, his family would face a prolonged interlude of horrifying, Dickensian destitution.

Through it all, Jim and Percy held onto a dream that helped get them through: one day, Jim Carrey was going to break through and earn the world's applause. And when that happened, the woes of the Carrey family would finally be over.

tHE **C**OMEDY **g**ENE

fROM EARLY childhood, Jim Carrey took on the special burden of providing comic relief to a troubled family. His father, Percy, worked as a bookkeeper, but he was also a frustrated performer who, as a teenager, had led a jazz band as well as playing saxophone and clarinet. Percy spent the rest of his life regretting that he had given up his show business career. It must have hit him hard that he was forced to sell his cherished sax in 1948 to pay the bills when his wife, Kathleen, gave birth to their first child, Patricia.

Jim was Percy and Kathleen's youngest child. The Carreys were a lower-middle-class Catholic family that bounced around the fringes of Toronto before and after Jim's birth in 1962. Jim's mother, Kathleen Marie Carrey—a former hairdresser—was the daughter of alcoholics who spent much of her life in bed taking painkillers and staring at a TV set. In their early years together, Kathleen—known to her friends as Kay and to her children as Mommsie—often sang with Percy's band. Later on, Kay's role within the family was to suffer and worry and issue warnings about dire consequences that had to be avoided. And she had reason to be worried concerning Percy Carrey's ability to be the sole provider for the family.

Percy was a gregarious character—a compulsive joke-teller whose patter provided a counterpoint to Kay's reticence. Yet beneath his flippant surface ran an undercurrent of tremendous sadness that his youngest child could not fail to detect. If life were fair, it seemed clear to Jim, Percy would be entertaining adoring crowds with his music and his patter.

Percy had French ancestry—the family name had been changed from Carré—but his pedigree wasn't enough to impress Kay's parents, who were constantly reminding him of his failures and made no secret of the fact that they thought he was a loser. Both Percy and Kay came from Catholic families in which education and money were in short supply. They married when they were both barely twenty years old and started their family soon afterward. Following the birth of Patricia, Kathleen had a series of miscarriages before giving birth in rapid succession to John, Rita and Jim.

James Eugene Carrey was born in Newmarket (thirty miles north of Toronto) on January 17, 1962, and spent most of his first four years in the nearby picturesque town of Aurora. Even while he was still in a high chair, Jim was known as a joker. If he didn't want to eat he would make all kinds of comical faces. To Percy, these were his son's first routines. Kay would warn him not to laugh because that would only encourage the child, but Percy couldn't help it, and he cheerfully admitted to a newspaper interviewer: "I guess I did encourage him. He says he gets it from me, and maybe that's true. I think it's better to go through life laughing instead of crying. If I ever stopped laughing, I'd probably kill myself."

Percy himself was known as a prankster who loved playing practical jokes on his children. Jim's sister Rita notes that every relative and old friend she has ever talked to makes a point of saying that Percy was a legendary cutup—the funniest man they ever met.

A frequent cause of family mayhem was a pet white mouse, which would often be allowed to escape from its cage, sending Kay into a tizzy. Even when the mouse was safely in its cage, the entire Carrey clan would often run rampant like a slapstick comedy troupe on the loose, indulging in spontaneous food-fights at the table or scaring passersby by donning weird costumes and running wild in the streets. Of the four children, the oldest, Patricia, was already married when Jim was growing up; John was shy, withdrawn and serious compared to Jim; and Rita was an outgoing, sociable girl but not nearly as manic as her younger brother. That left Jim clearly designated as the special Carrey offspring to whom Percy had passed on the comedy gene, the one best suited to compete with Dad for the title of funniest member of the Carrey family.

By the time Jim was ready to start school, his family had moved from Aurora to the Toronto suburb of Willowdale. Jim was enrolled at Blessed Trinity, the local Catholic school, where, he recalls: "I was quiet. I didn't have a friend in the world until I started hamming it up at the back of the class. That was the turning point. I realized I could do something silly and make people laugh, and then they'd want to talk to me."

A teacher named Mrs. Hays offered a glimpse of his future when she wrote on his report card: "Jim finishes his work first and then disrupts the class."

One day in grade three, sitting at the back during music class, he started to mimic the playing of a violin. The teacher noticed what was going on and challenged Jim to come up to the front and perform for the whole class. Jim went to the front of the class and did a weird dance, playing all of the Three Stooges—Larry, Curly and Moe. His schoolmates loved the act, and the teacher said, "Jim, that was really very good. How would you like to do it for the Christmas assembly?"

The next thing he knew, Jim was doing the Three Stooges for the entire school, but this time dressed as Santa Claus. The assembled students laughed hysterically, and the principal, Sister Mary John, invited him to take a curtain call. Then she announced: "Jim's pretty funny, isn't he? Jim wants to be a comedian when he grows up. Do you think he can do it?"

As far as eight-year-old Jim was concerned, his destiny was set from that moment on. As Carrey would explain to interviewers years later, his interest in performing emerged from just wanting to be special and be noticed. He had a distinctive look because of a chipped tooth, as a result of some playground scuffle. (Jim thought that was cool until he reached puberty, at which time, he later joked, "My penis said to me, 'You might want to get that fixed.'") He also had a Prince Valiant haircut, and was so thin that he was sometimes taunted as "Jimmy Gene the Stringbean." Jim didn't like being teased, but he learned how to stop others from laughing at him by laughing at himself first. He was a lonely boy without friends, and being funny was a way to earn recognition.

Jimmy, as he was often called in those days, realized that both of his parents were subject to spells of chronic depression, and his comedy could provide the antidote. His mission—to keep the family laughing—had a touching, selfless motive, but it was his devilish side that earned him the laughs. And those laughs were the reward he came to depend on—a sign that no matter what was going wrong, he had the power to make it all okay. Despite the family's serious problems, Jim never suffered from lack of love. There was always a strong feeling that members of the Carrey family stuck together and would always be there for one another. Occasionally Percy would wake Jim and say: "Your mother and I could use a good laugh—you're on in five."

Whether or not he realized it, Jim's manic behavior suggests that he relied on his comic diversions as a necessary tool for saving his parents from giving in to despair—maybe even as the price he needed to pay for the love and approval he craved and depended on, and especially for his status as Percy's favorite child.

Years later, Jim would tell a journalist that his mother was a professional sick person, always popping pills. According to her youngest child, this was Kay's method of gaining love and attention. According to Jim, the illnesses were "her medals." Jim would have to remind himself that, after all, Kay was the daughter of careless drunks who would leave her home alone at Christmas.

When Kay was in bed, with ailments real or imagined, Jim took on the challenge of amusing her and cheering her up. Among his favorite routines was his hilarious imitation of a praying mantis, which he performed in his underwear at her bedside, holding his elbows together. Fooling around in front of a mirror, he discovered that he had a special gift for mimicry and for transforming his face into different masks. Years later he told an interviewer: "You'd be amazed at how much fun you can have making faces."

For fresh material he turned to his favorite TV shows and movies. He practiced doing impressions of John Wayne, Don Addams and Frank Gorshin (who played the Riddler on TV's *Batman*). Once he learned to make his face look like someone famous, he would next try to get the voice to match. His first success was John Wayne. Jim was thrilled when Percy commented, "That sounds like John Wayne, all right."

A little later, Jim discovered that he could do singers, and he perfected the art of grinding his pelvis in the style of Elvis Presley and Tom Jones. Jim also discovered that you could get your revenge on annoying teachers and relatives by lampooning them for the amusement of others as soon as they were safely out the door. In the Carrey family it became a tradition that Jim would do an hour-long show every Christmas.

Without realizing it, Jim forged a link with the oldest traditions of screen comedy. He idolized Dick Van Dyke, a TV star who had been heavily influenced by the great comedians of silent movies, especially Buster Keaton. He was also drawn to Jerry Lewis. And at age ten, Jim sent his resumé to Carol Burnett, hoping to be discovered. One of his favorites, though, was James Stewart, an actor whose fame had little to do with hilarity. To the young Jim Carrey, the Jimmy Stewart of such movies as *It's a Wonderful Life*, *The Glenn Miller Story*, *Rear Window* and *The Spirit of St. Louis* represented something important. He was the good man who struggles with moral issues and is always rewarded for his virtue. The way Jim saw it, Jimmy Stewart was a lot like Percy Carrey—except that Percy had to struggle without the benefit of a Hollywood ending.

Percy tended to encourage Jim's shenanigans, but Kay found them alarming. She constantly warned him that he was going to the devil. When she got fed up, she would send him to his room, but he didn't mind; he could have a great time in front of his mirror.

Jim got into the habit of spending long hours alone, either in his bedroom or in a tiny closet he had cleared out to serve as his sanctuary. There he would practice making faces and doing impressions, but he also took up poetry, painting and drawing. For Jim, creativity and humor became a form of salvation. In discussing this childhood ritual many years later, Carrey described something like a trance-like concentration. "I was so lost in it, it was like being in the womb," he recalled. "It was like meditating or something; you don't care about anything."

Sometimes Kay would interrupt to ask Jim to take out the garbage or do some errand, and he would lose his temper and go berserk, knocking things off shelves. The message he was sending to his mother was: "Not now. Can't you see I'm in another world? Can't you see I'm creating?" Kay considered herself an expert in the saving of souls, but she had trouble understanding that Jim needed this sanctuary for his own preservation, and that to violate it was to invite his wrath and to risk watching him be transformed from Dr. Jekyll into Mr. Hyde.

O O O

WHEN JIM was nine, the Carrey family moved to Burlington, a town on Lake Ontario between Toronto and Hamilton. Percy had a job as bookkeeper, and later controller, at Aldershot Industrial Installations on Plains Road. The company was an offshoot of an older Aldershot firm which had long been in the business of renting mechanical and electrical equipment. It became apparent that many of the clients needing rented equipment also wanted a team of workers to do a job, and so the new firm was formed to exploit that opportunity by contracting the labor. Aldershot Industrial Installations, with several hundred employees, had a democratic flavor: it was partly management-owned and partly employee-owned.

Though the Carreys moved from one cramped apartment to another during these years, they would later look back on it as the family's happiest time. Patricia, the oldest of the four children, had already left home by the time the family moved. (Her name was now Patricia Mitchell, and before long she had three children.) The three Carrey siblings still at home transferred to Catholic schools in Burlington. Jim had a learning disability, dyslexia, but he learned to compensate by developing a phenomenal memory. And when Jim reached grade seven at St. Francis Xavier separate school in the fall of 1974, he got a lucky break. His teacher was Lucy Dervaitis. (Following a divorce years later, she would reclaim the name she'd had before her marriage, becoming known once again as Lucy Belvedere.)

Mrs. Dervaitis had moved to St. Francis from a school in a more affluent area, and she had been warned that she was entering a problem area. Aldershot was considered a rough district. It had a proliferation of dingy, tacky, low-rent townhouses and a less than stable population. Families drifted in and out of the neighborhood, and there was an unusually high turnover in the student population. It was obvious that many of the children had serious problems at home. Some looked as if they hadn't had the benefit of breakfast or a good night's sleep. One child at St. Francis was said to have been tied up in his family's basement for an extended period. A young thug was removed from the classroom of Mrs. Dervaitis after threatening her; some years later, he got his name into the local papers when he was charged with attempted murder.

Yet for Lucy Dervaitis, teaching was a sort of calling, and she embraced the challenge of reaching children other teachers had given up on. Sometimes she'd receive a note saying she had turned a child's life around, which made it all worthwhile. And the class she had for the 1974-75 school year (a mixture of grade-six and grade-seven kids) had the cream of the grade-seven crop.

Jim Carrey and Lucy Dervaitis were instant soulmates. From day one she found him a delightful character. And he was thrilled to win the approval of this important authority figure. "Other teachers might have regarded Jim as a disturbance and a pest," Lucy recalls. "I never found him a serious behavior problem. I don't even remember giving him detentions. I thought it was great that this funny little guy was showing such talent at a young age."

It was obvious that Jim craved attention. He loved making faces and doing impersonations (especially of some of the teachers at St. Francis) for the amusement of the other kids. A lot of teachers would have viewed this behavior as a rebelliousness that had to be crushed. Lucy Dervaitis took another approach. She asked Jim whether he would like to put together an act for the class. He was tremendously excited at the prospect, and entirely willing to comply with her conditions. Jim would be allowed to do his act at the end of the school day as long as he did his work and behaved well the rest of the time. This breakthrough was so important to Jim that he never forgot it.

Jim's act for the class would typically include an impression of Elvis (then in his late Vegas period) or John Wayne. There would also be a lot of goofy faces and much jumping around. For the rest of the class, the Jim Carrey show was a much-desired break from class-room routine. Whenever the other kids got bored, they'd petition Mrs. Dervaitis to let Jim do his act. Frequently she would refuse these requests, warning people to get down to work and stop trying to take advantage of her—Jim's act was for special occasions.

Jim was not only a performer, he was also a cartoonist. His gleeful sense of humor was apparent in a caricature of Mrs.

Dervaitis losing control of the class and handing out detentions. Today that cartoon is a cherished item in her Jim Carrey collection.

For Christmas in 1974, Jim was given a puppet he named Mr. Carrot Top, and he began developing a ventriloquist comedy act. He wound up using Carrot Top in an elocution contest sponsored by the local Optimists Club. At first Jim didn't know what his speech should be about. Mrs. Dervaitis suggested that since he was interested in comedy, he could talk about the history of humor. Filled with enthusiasm, Jim worked some of his comedy routines into the speech and included a big part for the dummy. He wound up taking first prize in the competition—a source of pride for years to come.

o o o

AT **ALDERSHOT** Industrial Installations, Percy Carrey occupied a tiny basement office. According to Fred Tharme, a vice-president of the company, the air in there was always blue because Percy was a chainsmoker, addicted to king-size Benson and Hedges. Percy handled all the company's financial affairs. "We'd provide input data for his records," recalls Tharme, "and he would tell us how the dollars had been spent so far on a project and tried to project the final cost based on the information he had available."

According to Tharme, Percy was a likable guy, popular among the office staff, and very expressive. "He had this big pointy chin," says Tharme, "and his eyes would light up. He was under a lot of pressure but he never bullied people. He would just say to the girls in the office, 'This has to be done by Friday.'"

Joanne Massey, one of Percy's assistants, thought he was a great guy. The better she got to know him, however, the more aware she became of his personal problems. Despite his easy, friendly manner, Percy had a lot on his mind. He was having problems at the office with the company management, and he had problems at home as well, she sensed. Percy's colleagues at work never saw any sign of Kay. She didn't even turn up at office parties. And Percy seemed to take on many of the domestic responsibilities—stopping on the way home to do grocery shopping at the local Busy Bee, or driving his children to and from their activities.

Joanne liked the fact that, regardless of office pressures, Percy regarded family as life's top priority. Joanne Massey recalls him fondly as "the only person I ever worked for who would push me out the door to go to my son's hockey game." Other bosses would insist you make up the time. Percy did not.

"Percy was proud of all his kids," Massey recalls, "but especially Jimmy. Jimmy was his pride and joy."

Joanne even took Jim to Peewee hockey tryouts, but as a prospective goalie he was no Johnny Bower. (Jim did play football on a local team for several seasons, and was known for making faces behind the coach's back and getting teammates to crack up.) Since Massey knew that Jim had a gift for doing impressions and Percy was eager to encourage Jim's talent as a performer, she invited them to meet her brother. He was a ventriloquist who had made a career of entertaining passengers on cruise ships but was now thinking of retiring and managing talented kids. Nothing much came of the encounter, but Percy seemed to enjoy the experience hugely. It gave him some ideas about Jim's potential future in show business—a dream that was starting to turn into an obsession.

hARD **t**IMES

IN 1976, **AT** the age of forty-nine, Percy was facing the greatest crisis of his life. At Aldershot Industrial Installations, company president Alfred Voytek had stepped aside (he would later become chairman of the board), and John Eindhoven took over. Important structural changes were being made. Percy's seemingly stable job was collapsing under him, and finding another steady job at this point in his life was not going to be easy.

Percy suddenly found himself out of a job, and a younger man was brought in to replace him. Some of his colleagues, including Fred Tharme and Joanne Massey, felt very sorry that Percy was being dealt this cruel blow after so many years with the firm, but their sentiments couldn't save his job.

According to Tharme (a vice-president of the firm at the time), changes in the operation of the company reflected the contrasting backgrounds and personalities of Voytek and Eindhoven. Voytek had served his apprenticeship as a tradesman and worked his way up. He was known as a tough taskmaster and a shrewd businessman of the old school. Eindhoven was less popular with some of the old hands, who considered him an interloper because he had come up through sales and marketing. He was a gregarious, ambitious operator who, according to Tharme, liked to put his own stamp on the operation by moving people around and shaking things up.

This is how Eindhoven recalls the former controller of Aldershot Industrial Installations: "Percy had some health problems, and he had difficulty coping with a variety of problems and employees. He was an old-fashioned pencil-and-paper bookkeeper, dealing with a situation that was difficult and complex. He had great difficulty coping with the constant high pressure. He had headaches and he was high-strung. The job was more than he could handle."

Under Eindhoven, the company abandoned its quarters on Plains Road and moved to a new building on North Service Road. A few years later, the company's bookkeeping system would be computerized, eliminating all the high pressure that had spelled Percy's downfall. But that irony was of no use to the Carrey family, all of whose lives were about to be forever scarred by the loss of Percy's job.

Looking back years later, Jim would think of Percy as a broken-hearted man. His father's sadness made such an impact on Jim that his life and career would proceed largely from his fierce determination not to wind up the same way. In the apprenticeship of Jim Carrey, the decline and fall of Percy overshadowed everything else. It was the catastrophe that gave Jim the motivation for everything he later achieved.

At the age of fifteen, Jim's life was taking a disturbing downward turn, and he found himself in the midst of a family melodrama that had more than a touch of Victorian Gothic—like something out of a Charles Dickens novel. When Aldershot

Industrial dumped Percy, the family tried at first to get by on emergency measures. Rita, who was sixteen at the time, turned her babysitting money over to Percy and Kay to buy groceries. And John, who was eighteen, contributed the paycheck from his part-time job to cover some of the family's bills. But as weeks turned into months and Percy failed to get a job equivalent to the one he had lost, the pressure mounted and the situation became more alarming. Before long, creditors were closing in and the Carreys were facing eviction. Percy needed not only a job but a place for the family to live.

Finally Percy made a desperate move. Titan Wheels, a factory in Scarborough (on the northeast fringe of Toronto) needed a night security man. Instead of simply taking the job himself, Percy worked out a weird arrangement. The entire family would work for the factory and would be given a place to live—a historic stone farmhouse, adjacent to the factory, called Weir House, which was owned by Titan.

The plant, which manufactured wheels for tractors and off-road equipment, was part of the Titan Proform Co. Ltd., operated by a prosperous Toronto businessman named Joe Tannenbaum as an offshoot of his Runnymede Development Co. What made Titan a valuable business was a certain exclusive technique for bending metal to form a wheel. The business had been moved to the Scarborough location in the mid-1970s, just before the Carreys arrived.

Tannenbaum had purchased Titan from Dufferin Material and Construction, a construction company, and later sold it to an American tycoon, Maury Taylor, who made millions through a shrewd leveraged buyout deal. Taylor, who once made a run for the Republican presidential nomination, bought the company for $32 million and flipped it not long afterward for a staggering $450 million.

How was it possible that such a high-flying company would exploit a destitute family by keeping them in conditions of poverty and servitude? According to Pat Bradley, who was general counsel to the firm, Percy was under such severe financial pressure that he arranged to have checks made out to his sons, John and Jim. In fact, it was Jim who signed the contract.

"It was a strange arrangement," Bradley recalls. "Percy seemed like a nice man, but he was very far down in his luck. He had lost his job and seemed rather desperate. I assumed that he had creditors hounding him and he was trying to prevent any money he might earn from falling into their hands."

Tannenbaum, now deceased, acted as president of the company, and he was known as a bit of an ogre. "The old man was very demanding," recalls Bradley. "He thought it would be more efficient to combine the janitorial, custodial and security jobs. Most of the work had to be done at night."

John, Rita and Jim all reported for work on the night shift at the factory. Percy spent all night as the security guard. Rita cleaned the offices upstairs while Jim and John did the cleaning on the factory floor downstairs, using industrial machines. They waxed, they polished, they dusted, they cleaned the toilets. There was no chore too scummy for them.

Jim could feel the mood darkening; there was an air of doom about the family. Looking back on this grim interlude years later, after he had achieved Hollywood stardom, Carrey recalled: "It was a horrendous time in my life. I hated everything and everybody. When you're a kid, something like this makes you mad at the world." He would ask himself: "How can the world do this to my dad? He's such a great guy, and this just isn't fair."

The worst part, as far as Jim was concerned, was that Percy had been hit by a double whammy. He had given up his dream of playing the saxophone for a band and settled instead for a safe job—only to have the safe job collapse. Seeing his dad do that kind of work tore Jim up. It made him realize that there is no such thing as social security. Jim promised himself he would never make the same mistake as Percy—giving up what he wanted to do with his life in favor of a steady job. The lesson Jim saw in Percy's predicament was this: no assurances are offered in this life, so you might as well do what you passionately want to do.

Living right next to the factory, the Carreys felt they were on call seven days a week, twenty-four hours a day. From time to time the children were encouraged to take a few days off, but Percy and Kay never went anywhere. According to Rita's account, this feeling of being trapped made the senior Carreys bitter and resentful.

For grade ten, Jim had transferred in the fall of 1977 from Aldershot High School in Burlington to a huge new high school, Agincourt Collegiate Institute. He was so exhausted from working an eight-hour night shift at the factory that he couldn't understand what his teachers were talking about. He had no friends and didn't want any. Deeply embarrassed about his family's appalling circumstances, he preferred to keep his distance from the other kids at school. Anyway, he had no time for a normal teenage social life. All he wanted to do was catch up on his sleep.

As soon as Jim turned sixteen in January 1978, he told Percy he had decided to quit school. Sitting in the security office at Titan, Percy shed a tear or two at the news, then pulled himself together and told Jim: "Well, you're sixteen. You're a man now. You've got to make your own decision."

By then the entire family seemed to be caught in the grip of a terrible anger. At Titan there were some ugly altercations involving East Indian and Jamaican co-workers, and the Carreys got drawn into them. What was erupting was something like a race war, and for a while it seemed to turn Percy and his children into bigots. Jim got into the habit of carrying a baseball bat on his cleaning cart, as if he were just waiting for someone to dare look at him the wrong way.

Many years later, Jim admitted that collective misery temporarily turned the Carrey family into monsters and racists. "I really understand how people who put themselves in a wrong situation in life can lose their soul and their spirit," he remarked.

Typically Jim would find his brother John expressing his frustration by taking a sledgehammer to a large cleaning machine and swearing loudly. Jim once threw a bench at a co-worker, and more than once put his fist through a wall. (Later he'd explain that the damage was done by a sweeping machine that had gone berserk.)

Still, the Carreys tried to keep their spirits up. Every Friday night the extended family—including Jim's married sister, Pat, with her husband and children, and Rita's Burlington boyfriend (later husband), Al Fournier— would go over to the factory's cafeteria. One of the big attractions there was the company's microwave oven. Kay would bring wieners and buns. Jim would entertain the gang, jumping from table to table doing a ballet spoof.

Around that time, Jim became determined to lose his virginity, and he looked to his future brother-in-law, Al Fournier, for instruction. Al coached him on such technical matters as how to massage a girl's nipples. Then one night Jim went to a party with John and Rita and was invited upstairs by a skinny twenty-five-year-old girl whose name he soon forgot. But he remembered years later that Styx's *Grand Illusion* was playing. After that night he never saw the girl again.

Finally, in the spring of 1978, the family had a soul-searching talk and decided that they just couldn't stand their life at Titan Wheels. The experience was doing awful things to them, turning them into people they didn't like. So they collectively made the decision to quit—even though none of them had another job, and they had nowhere to go.

At that point the Carrey family saga took an even more bizarre twist. Having no other roof over their heads, Percy, Kay, John, Rita and Jim moved into a beat-up yellow Volkswagen camper van. For eight months, they called that van home, parking it on campgrounds in the Toronto area. That summer they often drove the van to King City, where their daughter Pat Mitchell lived with her husband and three children, and pitched a tent on the Mitchells' lawn. For Jim, who loved to mythologize his life in terms of his favorite TV shows and movies, this was not merely a nasty experience, it was also a chance to explore what it might have been like to belong to the Joad family getting through the worst of the Great Depression in the 1940 movie *The Grapes of Wrath*.

Years later, after moving to Los Angeles, Jim Carrey turned this painful episode of his life into a comedy monologue. "I know a lot about the poor because we became homeless for a long time," he told audiences at the Comedy Store. Then he'd deliver the punchline: "It was in Canada, so I thought we'd just gone camping." He'd say his parents were so embarrassed that they'd try to convince their kids that nothing bad was happening. Sometimes Jim would ask, "Dad, are we by any chance living below the poverty line?" And the answer would be: "No, son, we're rich as long as we have each other. Now get into the dumpster."

Probably the first part of the joke was an accurate recollection—only the gag about the dumpster was invented to get a laugh.

The Carreys were living like gypsies, but they felt an over-whelming sense of liberation. After escaping from their grotesque situation at Titan Wheels, they felt almost giddy and carefree—and much happier than they had been doing jobs they hated. Maybe living out of a van wasn't anyone's ideal. But their mood lightened. Once again, jokes and laughter became an ongoing part of Carrey family life. Once again, they felt free enough to be silly—to indulge in such favorite rituals from the old days as Sunday night food-fights. And during the summer of 1978, various members of the family, one by one, ventured out into the world and found jobs.

At this point in his life, however, Jim's limited credentials left him trapped in the world of blue-collar workers. After all, he had dropped out of school with nothing better than a grade-nine education. As for his dreamed-of comedy career, his inauspicious debut at Yuk-Yuk's two years earlier had left him shattered and reluctant to repeat such a painful experience. He hadn't given up his dream, and he'd promised himself he would make it come true one day, but for now it was on hold.

That's why Jim Carrey, at age sixteen, took a job at Oxford Picture Frame in Richmond Hill (just north of Toronto) making fibreglass insulation and picture frames. His job entailed feeding pieces of wood into a painting machine. "I'm amazed they didn't fire me the first day," he recalled later. "I was terrible at the job. I'm useless doing things with my hands."

To his fellow workers, Jim was a popular recruit. He was constantly hamming it up and keeping the other guys in stitches. But to the factory foreman, Jim's behavior was no laughing matter. Once again, he was acting like that troublesome kid whose teachers accused him of disrupting the rest of the class. At the Richmond Hill factory, there was a great deal more laughter and high spirits with Jim Carrey on the scene than there had been before, but there was also an alarming decline in productivity. His foreman was not pleased. After six months, Jim Carrey's days as a factory worker came to an end once and for all.

Meanwhile, the Carrey family had moved out of the camper van and secured a very modest place to hang their hats—a brown winterized cottage in the popular summer resort of Jackson's Point on Lake Simcoe, just an hour's drive north of Toronto, and much closer to their old home in Aurora than they'd been for years. Unlike their neighbors, the Carreys lived in Jackson's Point year-round, surrounded by summer cottages of people whose principal residences were in the city.

The Carrey family had put their collective nightmare behind them, but for Jim the scars would never quite heal. He would have to deal with terrible memories for years to come, possibly for the rest of his life. He had been robbed of a normal teenager's life, and there was a price to be paid for that loss. As well, his intellectual development was impeded by having to take on the world with a grade-nine education—leaving him in the position of feeling he always had to play catch-up with his peers.

Nevertheless, the hard knocks Jim learned to endure in the Carreys' darkest period undoubtedly propelled him to the spectacular success he eventually achieved. "The bad times make you feel you deserve the good stuff," he once explained. His greatest bursts of creativity were born out of desperation; so was his remarkable willingness to take risks.

It took a long time before Jim Carrey was ready to face the huge impact of what he had gone through. For years he simply didn't talk about it. Even people who considered themselves close to him in the early 1980s knew little or nothing of the saga. And though many of the stand-up comics of the era liked to show off their hostility, Jim Carrey seemed refreshingly free of anger—a sweet, polite, old-fashioned kid who was almost unfailingly courteous, clean-cut and eager to please. As he explained in an interview years afterward, "My focus is to forget the pain of life—to mock it and reduce it."

In the meantime, he cast himself in the role of family healer. Not only would he make other members of the Carrey clan laugh, he would use his talent to support the family. Winning the hearts of audiences would not only make him feel special, it would somehow assuage the pain and humiliation Percy and Kay had endured. His success would be their payback. Reversing the usual routine of parents trying to protect their children from feeling the sting of the world's cruelty, Jim Carrey took on the impossible burden of cancelling the suffering of his parents.

It would be eight to ten years before Carrey was ready to acknowledge the pain and anger he'd tried to bury, and begin letting his demons emerge, both offstage and on. By then he was ready to accept the one point about his life that might seem the most obvious: his was not the kind of adolescence that anyone really ever gets over.

four

o o o o o

joining the Club

IN HIS SPARE time, Jim spent hours in front of a mirror practicing his impressions. Percy was nudging him to get back onstage again. It would be a mistake, he told his son, to give up the dream of becoming a comedian just because of one bad night at Yuk-Yuk's. After all, you couldn't expect everyone to like your stuff all the time. And they could work on the script and the impressions, change things around, try out new material. Working on Jim's routine, father and son would try to top each other, trading lines they considered killingly funny. Kay sometimes let them know she thought a certain bit of material was dreadful—which led Percy and Jim to refer to her sarcastically as the Rex Reed of the family.

One night Percy arranged for Jim to appear on the Kinsmen charity telethon on a small-town cable channel. He even managed to get Jim his first paying gig—an appearance at a restaurant called the Hayloft in Scarborough, for which Jim was paid twenty dollars. By mid-1978 it was time for a return to the bigtime— Yuk-Yuk's Komedy Kabaret in downtown Toronto.

A lot of things had changed in the two and a half years since Jim's traumatic experience in the basement on Church Street. Yuk-Yuk's was no longer a once-a-week novelty. After becoming so popular that hundreds of would-be patrons were often lined up on the sidewalk, unable to get in, the club had secured a permanent, full-time home.

The weekly show caught the attention of Jack Kapica, an arts reporter for the *Globe and Mail*, who was intrigued by the frenzied atmosphere. During an interview over dinner before the show, Kapica found club owner Mark Breslin amiable, intelligent and articulate. But when Breslin walked onto the stage as master of ceremonies, he turned into a different person, according to Kapica, "as if he were consumed by juvenile hysteria."

Most of the acts were excruciatingly terrible, getting by on bad taste rather than talent, but the customers seemed energized, enjoying the worst performers more than the almost-good ones. To Kapica, this was a night from hell, but it was also a good story. His feature article got a prominent spot in the weekend edition, accompanied by a striking cartoon featuring a pimply-faced comic. The publicity was a break for Yuk-Yuk's (which had no advertising budget) and helped the club become known.

Breslin had tapped a new audience—people in their teens and twenties who considered themselves too knowing to swallow the soft, sentimental conventions of old-fashioned popular entertainment. Breslin's own sensibility was right in sync with the prevailing aesthetic of the period—hip cynicism. It was stand-up comedy rather than sketch comedy that interested Breslin, and he didn't make the mistake of aiming too high. Toronto's Second City Company had been established at the Old Firehall and was now about to reach the TV screen with a series called *SCTV*, but to

Breslin's way of thinking, Second City's brand of revue humor was too tame.

"We were flirting with the punk notion that show business stinks," Breslin recalls. "It followed that bad is just as good as good. So we weren't afraid of having bad acts. We had our share of real losers, but they contributed to the charm of the place."

As of March 1978, Yuk-Yuk's was a booming, full-time club in the fashionable Yorkville area of Toronto. Sensing that the comedy scene was about to explode, Breslin had taken over a space at 1280 Bay Street that had previously housed three boutiques. The place was a dump, but he knew his audience would be comfortable with tackiness. He had everything painted black. No liquor was served. The customers didn't seem to mind. They were happy to munch cookies and guzzle soft drinks. The cover charge went up from two dollars to four dollars—six dollars on weekends. On busy nights there were two shows. According to Ralph Benmergui (then an aspiring young comic, who later became a prominent CBC television host), the opening of the new club ushered in "a fantastically exciting time for all of us."

The club was becoming more professional. There was even some planning about who would appear and in what order. Larry Horowitz, who was already well known as a polished stand-up comic by then, recalls: "When the Yorkville club opened, we were all in the same boat, just hoping to attract enough customers to keep the place open." According to Horowitz, there were perhaps eleven comedians appearing on an average night, and often six of them were good enough to headline. Every day, it seemed, someone new wandered in.

Audiences were attracted to Yuk-Yuk's by the promise that the rules of polite society would be dropped, and the shams as well.

Nothing was sacred, except the art of getting off a good line. Breslin, who would serve as emcee at least once week, was a well-dressed lord of misrule—a not-so-genial ringmaster who'd smile at the crowd and point out: "After the show a lot of you will be going home to sleep with people you don't really love."

The system at Yuk-Yuk's required newcomers to make a number of appearances in the late-night slot reserved for amateurs. There was no pay for amateurs, just the tantalizing prospect of future glory. And an awful lot of hopefuls turned up. One of them was Jim Carrey, who had not yet marked his seventeenth birthday. According to Bruce Harriott, then working at Yuk-Yuk's as a manager, Carrey was a fresh-faced, tall and skinny teenager with a huge talent that was immediately apparent. Jim Carrey was already more polished and more sure of himself than the kid who had been humiliated two years earlier in the basement room on Church Street. Carrey reminded Harriott of Robin Williams, who dropped into Yuk-Yuk's one night around this time: "Both had a childlike quality. When they'd go into their act, find their persona, they became completely free, as if to say 'I'm into my own thing now. You can watch me if you like.'"

Unlike the other young comics trying to break in at Yuk-Yuk's, Carrey wasn't a social critic, and there was nothing dark or edgy about his act. He wasn't trying to be clever or cerebral, and he wasn't doing satiric material about the frustration of dating or the hypocrisy of TV commercials. He didn't show off his neuroses, like some of the other comedians. He seemed almost unbelievably polite and clean-cut, and professional in an old-fashioned way. His benignly goofy act wasn't about being smart and wised up; it was about old-school clowning. His credo might have been the song *Make 'Em Laugh* sung by Donald O'Connor in *Singin' in the Rain*.

Jim Carrey specialized in humorous impressions, but he was willing to do anything if he thought it would get a laugh—pratfalls, making funny faces, striking poses, twisting his body into weird shapes. What Bruce Harriott remembers about Carrey in those early days was his intense physicality. Like Dustin Hoffman and Laurence Olivier, he seemed to create a character by first discovering the appropriate gestures, twitches and body shapes.

Eleanor Goldhar, who was working on publicity and bookkeeping for Breslin, remembers Carrey as an unusually quiet person compared to the other aspiring comics: "You could see him watching and listening—observing closely, paying attention to everything that was going on." Suzette Couture—later a hugely successful screenwriter, but in those days working as a comedy performer—was struck by the neediness in Jim Carrey's personality. To Couture, Carrey had the look of someone living in poverty. The first time she saw him he was wearing a weird jacket that didn't quite fit; the sleeves were much too short. "He seemed desperate to succeed and be loved, and there was a sense of tragedy underlying what he wanted from the audience," she recalls.

Carrey learned fast. He not only graduated from the amateur section to prime-time; he began to attract a following. Yuk-Yuk's in the late 1970s had become a feverish hothouse where all things seemed possible. Breslin and his staff cleverly made every aspect of the business into a gag. The menu was full of jokes, the special dessert consisted of pornographic gingerbread people, and the company checks featured punchlines (which the club's bank agreed to print with considerable reluctance). As Eleanor Goldhar puts it, comics tended to be like homeless people, and the club turned into a kind of halfway house where they could hang out at all hours of the day and night.

In this atmosphere, a number of people enjoyed the feeling that they might suddenly grasp power, fame and success—and some of them were ascending quickly. Among the regulars were Horowitz, Sheila Gostick, a kid named Howie Mandel, Steve Brinder, Marla Lukofsky and Benmergui's friends Paul K. Willis and Michael Boucoeur, who had an act called La Troupe Grotesque. And there was Katie Ford, who was even younger than Jim Carrey. Appearing at Yuk-Yuk's when she was fourteen, Ford had a highly developed sense of the absurd. By the time she was sixteen, she was one of the regular writers contributing to the ABC weekly sitcom *Growing Pains.*

Hostility was the electricity that made the place hum. Abusing a member of the audience, Breslin would remark: "Puke-green is really your color, isn't it?" Or if he was heckled, he'd retort: "You know, I could urinate that far."

The way Ralph Benmergui remembers it, comedy for these guys wasn't exactly a business or a job; it was a calling. You did this because you loved it. Benmergui, who had moved out of his parents' house, was paying seventy-five dollars a month to sleep on a friend's couch. Around this period, he was appearing in a band, which required him to be on the road many nights. But whenever he was in town Benmergui loved to hang out at the club. For one thing, you could watch other comedians and learn from them. And according to Benmergui, "You hung out to get dates, and to get high."

If you got hungry and had no money for food, you could slip into the kitchen and grab a scoop of something on a bagel. It was understood that a lot of people had a kind of mystical belief that comedy was their life. Since there was no money in it for many of them, it became part of Breslin's role to help them avoid starvation. Breslin was part exasperating taskmaster, part solicitous Jewish mother nourishing his boys and reminding them, figuratively speaking, not to go out on a cold night without a scarf. That's one reason comics would return to Yuk-Yuk's even when they had more lucrative gigs elsewhere. This was a place where they knew they belonged.

The first genuine star to emerge at Yuk-Yuk's soon after the move to Yorkville was Howie Mandel, who managed to make a career out of infantile silliness. Mandel drew big laughs by portraying a baby, using a diaper and baby hat as props. He would stand on the stage squealing "What? What? What?" And the audience would get hysterical. Mandel could even get a laugh by taping a potato chip to his jacket.

Like Carrey, Mandel specialized in physical stunts rather than verbal brilliance; like Carrey, he was appealingly childlike and eager to be loved and admired. But unlike Carrey, who always seemed vulnerable, Mandel had had a privileged upbringing, and he brought a sense of entitlement to the stage. For Jim, Howie Mandel provided an important road-marker on the path that Carrey wanted to take: Mandel was able to use his success at Yuk-Yuk's as a springboard to a Hollywood career.

The same year that Jim Carrey became a Yuk-Yuk's regular, a brilliant and abrasive comedian named Mike MacDonald arrived by bus from Ottawa. Breslin had discovered him at an Ottawa club, and he quickly turned MacDonald into a featured headliner. There were dozens of comics turning up at the club every week, and many of them were scarcely noticed by Breslin. Mike MacDonald was one of the few that Breslin got truly excited about.

"Mike was the person who leaped off the stage and epitomized the aesthetic I was trying to create," Breslin says. "He had more talent than anyone who ever came through Yuk-Yuk's. He would stare into the abyss and filter what he found through his own brain. He was just amazing. He could make people laugh and make them feel at the same time."

If there was one performer destined for stardom, almost everyone who was around at the time would have said it was Mike MacDonald. Instead, his destiny was to play Salieri to Jim Carrey's Mozart. MacDonald had a subversive wit; he was edgy, he was vicious, he was an original, and he was completely unpredictable. And there seemed to be a breathtaking connection between MacDonald's brilliance on stage and the recklessness of his personal behavior. After hours, MacDonald was the unofficial leader of those who liked to live on the wild side—comics who found some of the after-hours parties a little too tame. MacDonald and his core group of half a dozen followers would leave these gatherings and go off to hang out on their own until the sun came up. MacDonald's festivities often included not only serious drinking but acid trips and eventually heroin. It wasn't until years later, after he'd moved to L.A., that MacDonald gave up liquor and drugs and came to terms with the fact that he was a manic-depressive.

Compared to Mike MacDonald, Jim Carrey seemed like Rebecca of Sunnybrook Farm. MacDonald, who made no attempt to hide his opinion of his colleagues, was scornful of Howie Mandel and would often make disparaging remarks about him, sometimes to his face. He was more tolerant of Carrey. The consensus among the smart and the hip was that Carrey was polished and entertaining in a vulgar Las Vegas sort of way. He was a bit too square and mainstream to win their admiration and respect, but they recognized his knack for pleasing audiences.

Mark Breslin's own appreciation of Carrey was limited. He

could see that Carrey was winning ovations from the audience, but he couldn't comprehend why an aspiring young comic would bother doing impressions of performers like James Stewart, who were considered boring and conventional by Breslin and his friends. That was the sort of stuff you expected to see in a tuxedo at the glitzy lounge of a convention hotel, not at a hip downtown comedy club.

Breslin was a wised-up urban Jew who liked Woody Allen movies and Philip Roth novels. He had certain ideals about what kind of comedy he wanted to promote. Lenny Bruce and Mort Sahl were among his heroes, and Jim Carrey's act was about as far off that track as you could get. Carrey epitomized values—rural, square and deeply Gentile—that were completely alien to Breslin and his crowd. Breslin was drawn to people who proudly displayed their neuroses like badges and traded witty put-downs; Carrey was so unfailingly courteous that Breslin felt little kinship with him.

There was a great divide between Carrey and some of the other regulars at Yuk-Yuk's. Most of them were downtown people who understood the environment because they lived not far from the club. Carrey was driving down from Jackson's Point, and it might as well have been another planet. It would have been a leap for Yuk-Yuk's insiders to embrace Carrey, even if it weren't for an additional barrier: when he first became a regular, Jim Carrey was often accompanied by his father. Percy Carrey was very garrulous, and when he hung around the club in his threadbare suits, pumping the hands of Breslin and others, people thought he was wired and speedy. Percy was by far the oldest person on the scene, and his presence was slightly embarrassing. The hip kids didn't quite know what to make of him.

At this point, Percy was the closest thing Jim had to a manager, but his presence was making things awkward. Jim finally went through the painful exercise of explaining to him that it wasn't cool for a young comic at a club to have his father hanging around. Having missed out on a normal teenage life, Jim was more than ready to have a good time. He was starting to make friends, and he could see that Percy was an impediment to his social life.

Everyone who knew Jim Carrey could see he had talent, but Percy Carrey's encouragement went way beyond normal paternal pride. His aggressive promotion of Jim carried unnerving echoes of Mama Rose, the nightmarish mother of Gypsy Rose Lee and June Havoc, as portrayed by Ethel Merman in the musical *Gypsy*.

Some nights Jim Carrey did not return to Jackson's Point. He would often crash at the apartment of his friend Avi Koren, a short, bald Israeli who worked as a cook at a Middle-Eastern restaurant called Yofi's. Koren also became Jim's sound man, taking charge of the tapes used in Jim's act. For a couple of years, they seemed inseparable.

According to Joel Axler, Carrey would often wind up playing Monopoly in the middle of the night. And it was obvious Carrey had a head for business; he was the most dazzling Monopoly player Axler had ever met.

Jim Carrey was clearly enjoying his first taste of success and independence. His high spirits seemed to spill out of him, and his life had the manic flavor of an endless comedy performance. Carrey was hungry for attention, ready for adventure and eager to learn from anyone he encountered. The sound of an ovation from a happy audience was a drug he couldn't get enough of. It had effectively drowned out the painful memory of his Yuk-Yuk's initiation. As for the traumatic experiences he had endured over the past few years, especially at Titan Wheels, he preferred not to talk about that. Other comics could vent their anger and share their dark side with the audience. Jim Carrey preferred to present himself as just a sweet, goofy, rubber-faced kid who could keep audiences happy by making them laugh.

fIVE

○ ○ ○ ○ ○

fUNNY bUSINESS

gIVEN THE explosion of stand-up comedy in the late '70s, it was inevitable that some of the comedians at Yuk-Yuk's would get offers to appear elsewhere. Mark Breslin was fiercely protective of what he regarded as his exclusive turf, and he took the view that the performers to whom he had given a break owed him nothing less than total loyalty. He did not want his performers to work at clubs competing with Yuk-Yuk's, but he was happy to see his regulars doing gigs that were no threat to his interests.

One night in 1979, Jim Carrey accompanied Ralph Benmergui to a rowdy bar in Toronto's west end called the Queensbury Arms. Paul K. Willis and Michael Boucoeur of the comedy duo La Troupe Grotesque had a regular Monday night gig there—a wet T-shirt contest. On this particular Monday, they couldn't make it, and they asked their friend Benmergui to fill in. The gig, which paid a fee of $200, required two performers. While one was on stage revving up the audience and asking for volunteers, the other would go out into the crowd and come back with recruits. They had to be hosts, they had to do some comedy routines, and they had to organize the con-tests. Women would have their shirts sprayed with water until their breasts were showing; men would pull down their pants and dis-play their butts through their underwear.

Benmergui asked Carrey to share the gig with him. Ralph would take $150 because he was the established performer, leaving $50 for Jim, who was just coming off amateur night. The two of them drove out together in a powder-blue Volkswagen Beetle owned by Percy and Kay.

The Queensbury turned out to be a bigger and rougher bar than they had expected. "You go up there and entertain them for fifteen minutes while I work the room," Benmergui instructed Carrey.

The kid from Jackson's Point tried to win the boisterous folk over with his somewhat off-the-wall impression of Elvis as a victim of Thalidomide (this was two years after Elvis had died), but the crowd was having none of it. There was no hook at this place, but Jim Carrey bombed as thoroughly as he had on Church Street. He found it very upsetting, and Benmergui felt sorry for him. But driving back downtown, they found consolation in one thing: at least they had picked up a bit of cash for their trouble.

On another occasion, Carrey accompanied Larry Horowitz on a long drive to a gig in the suburbs, where Carrey was booked as the opening act and Horowitz was the featured headliner. Jim filled the time by doing impressions of Elmer Fudd and Porky Pig. "I remember thinking Jim was a nice kid but not exactly a real person," says Horowitz (who still works as a comic, now often earning large fees on the corporate circuit). "He seemed more like a living cartoon—half fairy tale, half animation—straight from Toontown. I thought that if a cartoon mated with a human and had a child, their baby would be Jim Carrey. And I had the feeling he would either self-destruct or else become very famous."

Leatrice Spevack had no doubt that Jim Carrey was going to become very famous. Spevack, a striking and fast-talking Yuk-Yuk's employee, had got into the comedy business through her ex-husband, Paul K. Willis (of La Troupe Grotesque), and she soon became a person Breslin relied on to spot talent. She started working evenings at the Yuk-Yuk's box office while spending her days as an assistant to Tony Molesworth, a comedian and juggler who sometimes appeared at the club. As a result of trying to arrange work for Molesworth, she got into the business of booking comedians.

Breslin was shrewd enough to recognize a business opportunity when he saw one, so he set up a talent-booking agency called Funny Business as a spinoff to his comedy club, and he put Spevack in charge of it. She would arrange for comedians to work at corporate meetings, for example, or perform at a university campus or a home for elderly people. Whenever these gigs were arranged through Funny Business, Breslin's company would get a percentage of the fee.

Spevack demonstrated her knack for recognizing talent when she quickly identified Jim Carrey as a star of the future. "The first time I saw Jim on stage," she recalls, "he had long hair and a T-shirt. He was a scraggly, messy-looking kid. He did singing impressions and a lot of pratfalls and goofy jokes. His jokes (mostly written by his father) were just terrible. And he was really raw and clearly needed a lot of work. But there was something about Jim that struck me—a certain magic.

"The next time I saw him he had cleaned up. He had cut his hair. He was wearing a blazer with gray flannel pants. This wasn't stylish dressing; he had a Sunday school look. He just seemed so clean and fresh and young that no matter how jaded you were, you could buy into what he was doing. His singing impressions, such as Elvis and Kermit the Frog, were so outstandingly poignant they could bring a tear to the eye. Despite the roughness of his routine, it was obvious the boy was teeming with talent and energy. More than that, Carrey had IT—that crazy indefinable quality that separates true stars from mere flashes. Call it magnetism. Call it charisma. Whatever you call it, he had it."

Spevack brought her excitement over Carrey to Breslin's attention, only to discover that Breslin was not terribly interested in the kind of material Carrey was doing. To Breslin, verbal comedy was an art form, but doing showbiz impressions was merely a party trick requiring craftsmanship. He criticized Carrey for pandering to the audience: if he wasn't getting a big response with his material, he would suddenly fall down—and the audience would laugh. Spevack shared Breslin's preference for an edgier, more satiric style of comedy, but she also felt that was beside the point. "It wasn't a matter of my taste or Mark's taste," she explains. "It was a matter of 'This guy's got it, he is really something, his talent is sensational.' And that's true whether or not his act is a reflection of your sensibility."

Even as Jim became a favorite at Yuk-Yuk's, Leatrice lined up other bookings for him. The comedy business was still in its infancy, so there were not many comedy clubs around, and there was little call for stand-up comics on TV. Still, she managed to send Jim to university campuses and police associations, to banquet halls and bars where he was too young to be served a drink. He was so charmingly naive and warm that his appeal extended beyond the narrow confines of comedy clubs. There was a certain gulf between Leatrice and Jim—she regarded him as a simpleminded country boy who came from a world she hardly knew—but she could see that he was going places. And she enjoyed trying to help him get there.

Jim was ingratiating and eager to please, and people liked him. He clearly didn't fit into Mike MacDonald's crowd or Mark Breslin's circle, but he made friends, such as the young comic Shawn Thompson. Surprisingly, the strongest and longest-lasting friendship he formed was a rather unlikely one with a veteran comedian named Wayne Flemming. What made them an odd couple was the fact that Flemming, who was already totally bald, was fourteen years older than Carrey.

A former disc jockey and draftsman from Nova Scotia, Flemming was considered an amusing hell-raiser. He was famous for his Jack Nicholson routine, and there was a touch of Nicholson in his personality. He was a veteran of the old days, before comedy clubs, when he shared the stage in frontier Ontario towns with a musical duo called Lisle. He loved to tell stories about his dangerous escapades on the touring circuit—both onstage and in the bedroom. In Owen Sound, he'd had a bottle thrown at him by someone in the audience, causing a wound that required several stitches to close. The rapport this road warrior established with the new lad from Jackson's Point led Leatrice to quip that Wayne was playing Falstaff to Jim's Prince Hal. When Wayne was around, you could expect crazy fun; that's what drew Jim to him.

Wayne, who had already been married and divorced by the time he met Jim, was a fan of Groucho Marx and loved doing Groucho's shtick, raising his eyebrows for comic effect and using cigars as hilarious props. In fact he had actually changed his name to Flemming as an homage to Erin Flemming, an auburn-haired actress from Ontario who had become Groucho's rather alarming companion (taking control of his life and his affairs) when Marx was in his dotage. There were plans for a movie about Groucho, and Wayne wanted the leading role.

Like Carrey, Flemming was a rambunctious country boy rather than one of the new breed of urban, intellectual comedians. The very first time he saw Jim perform, Wayne was knocked out by the level of talent and polish in the newcomer. He could see that Jim needed someone to take him in hand and show him around, and Wayne was the right guy for the task. For Jim, this entertaining new friend was not only someone to hang around with after the show, but a seasoned survivor whose judgment he could trust in such crucial areas as testing new material and understanding the politics of the comedy world. Jim felt he could trust Wayne and rely on him.

Wayne's friendship was just what Jim needed, because it gave him another older male figure as an alternative to Percy. Much as Jim adored his father, it was an embarrassment to have him constantly in tow. It made Jim cringe when Percy talked boastfully about Jim's achievements in front of him. Percy's enthusiasm came across as over-the-top, and it just wasn't cool. For Wayne, it was a source of great satisfaction to be chosen as mentor by the child prodigy of the comedy world. And of course Wayne passed on to Jim what he thought he had learned about women—at a time when Jim's sexual opportunities were expanding rapidly thanks to his success on stage.

Wayne and Jim were high-spirited playmates who operated on the same wavelength. Jim was given to bursts of creative energy in the middle of the night, and he liked company. He and Wayne enjoyed staying up all night together—walking along Bloor Street and talking, playing Monopoly, riding the subway in search of oddball characters they could mimic, or going up to Fran's restaurant on St. Clair Avenue West (open 24 hours) for grilled-cheese sandwiches with ketchup. On occasion, Jim and Wayne's late show featured more dramatic, action-packed escapades. One night, the two hyperactive, insomniac clowns let off some steam at four o'clock in the morning when they jumped the fence at Varsity Stadium on the University of Toronto's downtown campus, and tore around the track. Any bypasser would have been bewildered by this rampage, but they were actually making up a comedy routine. Jim had suddenly and spontaneously assumed the role of a washed-up champion decathlete locked out of the scene of his former glory.

0   0   0

JIM CARREY'S honeymoon with Yuk-Yuk's came to a nasty end in the early months of 1980 when he accepted a tempting offer to perform at a Montreal comedy club called Stitches. This was right around the time that Breslin was expanding with a chain of comedy clubs, starting with one in Montreal. Breslin was furious over what he regarded as a blatant case of disloyalty and ingratitude. But as far as Jim was concerned, he was, at the age of nineteen, the bread-winner for his family, and he simply couldn't afford to turn down a solid paying gig. Mark made it clear that there was a price to be paid: Jim Carrey was no longer to be booked into Yuk-Yuk's. Thus began a period of exile when Carrey seemed to be performing everywhere *except* Breslin's club.

During this period, Breslin was becoming increasingly embat-tled. The business was going through a slump, so he had to change his mind about serving liquor. A licenced restaurant-bar was opened adjacent to the club. Though it had the desired effect of increasing revenue, some people, including many of the top comedians appearing there, felt the atmosphere at Yuk-Yuk's was never again as good as it had been in the old, boozeless days. Meanwhile, a number of Breslin's employees had quarreled with him and moved on. Even if they felt emotionally tied to Yuk-Yuk's, they found themselves in the position of teenagers craving independence. The longer they put off leaving, the more they found Mark controlling, autocratric and hard to get along with.

Jim Carrey made no secret of the fact that he felt he had been unfairly treated. He and Wayne had a running gag about Mark. They liked to pretend that they were planning to open a chain of comedy clubs, each one next door to a Yuk-Yuk's. The object of this fantasy venture was to put Mark out of business.

In fact, Flemming did have a club to run. The owners of Tickles, a comedy club in Barrie (only minutes away from the Carrey cottage in Jackson's Point), hired him to be emcee and manager. And Jim quickly became the number-one performer there. The clientele at Tickles was very different from the Yuk-Yuk's crowd. According to Bill Brioux, a Toronto journalist and former comedian who once worked at Flemming's club, there would be lots of people from the nearby army base in the audience, and it was the sort of rough crowd in which throwing ashtrays at the performers was an accepted practice. Wayne knew how to play to this crowd. His act was scatological, and one of his favorite bits was to dress up as a flamboyant homosexual and prance around the stage using exaggerated effeminate gestures. He loved to be heckled, because that gave him a chance to heckle back. A tough guy in the crowd might shout "Dickhead!" at Flemming, and he would retort: "The lab called. Your brain is ready."

Even in this rough-and-tumble environment, Jim maintained a tone of graciousness and civility. John Gunn, a Toronto TV producer, recalls not only the brilliance of Carrey's act at Tickles but his surprisingly courtly manner. Jim would be dressed in a suit and tie, and at the end of a performance he would stand at the door chatting with members of the audience as they left.

Another comedy club where Jim often performed in 1980 was a new Toronto spot called Giggles, on Eglinton Avenue West near Bathurst. Jim was appearing at Giggles when he was approached by Leatrice Spevack, who had quit her job at Yuk-Yuk's after a disagreement with Breslin and was now planning to develop a career managing artists. Spevack's boyfriend at the time knew someone who was a manager for rock-and-roll bands, and suggested she could get a job with his company. That's how she began to work for Demi Thompson, whose firm, Square Sun Productions, handled a number of bands.

Though Thompson was mainly interested in musicians, Spevack suggested to him that the company could also take on some comedians. This was a field in which she had some expertise, and there was one young comedian she was particularly high on: Jim Carrey. One night she brought her prospective boss to see Jim's act at Giggles. Demi was not all that enthusiastic, according to Leatrice, but he agreed to give her a job at his agency and let her bring Carrey along as her first client. For Jim, who had never had a real manager (unless you count Percy), the arrangement offered some hope of career advancement at a difficult time—when he was feeling the pain of his exile from Yuk-Yuk's.

Leatrice fervently believed in Jim's talent, and she sensed he had the potential to become a star. But it wasn't going to happen while he was appearing at Tickles and Giggles. Jim needed a buildup, he needed major press coverage, and he needed to be placed in the best possible venue. In Canada, there was really only one place that could happen: Yuk-Yuk's in Yorkville.

Consequently, Leatrice undertook negotiations with her former boss, Mark Breslin, about getting a showcase week for Carrey at the Toronto club. Jim would play every night for a full week, he would be the featured headliner, and Leatrice would have a chance to get Toronto entertainment journalists out to take a good look at him.

But Breslin was still steamed about Carrey's appearance at the rival club in Montreal. He insisted that there was only one way he would give Carrey his showcase week in Toronto. First, Jim would have to appear for a week with no fee at the Yuk-Yuk's club in Montreal, as a kind of penance.

At first Jim balked at the condition, which was a form of punishment and humiliation—a ritual of making a very public bow of apology to Mark for being such a bad boy. But much as Jim resented the whole exercise, Leatrice talked him into it. And a couple of months later, in February 1981, Breslin made good on his pledge by bringing Carrey back to the Yorkville club for a week-long headline engagement. Almost from the moment Jim Carrey walked back onto that stage, it seemed clear that this was going to be a turning point in his career.

bREAKTHROUGH

JIM CARREY knew there was a lot riding on his week-long engagement at Yuk-Yuk's in late February 1981, and he was determined to make his return to Yorkville a personal triumph. At the age of nineteen, he was well prepared to make the second comeback of his career; he was now a more polished performer than he had been at his last appearance there a year earlier. Never known for coasting on old accomplishments, Carrey was constantly adding new material, staying current, spending hours in front of the mirror, looking for fresh inspiration.

Indeed, the process of creating his impressions was a strange, ongoing form of osmosis. Jim was the first to admit that he didn't quite understand how he did it. Sometimes he would get the voice first, and then the face would come later. He might be listening to a vocalist on a record, singing along, and then a few hours later the precise voice that he would do onstage would suddenly come to him. It was as if, he confided to an interviewer, he had been asleep while an instructional record was speaking to his subconscious. As for the face, once the right voice came to Jim, he could feel his facial muscles clicking in to match.

Other times he would be fooling around in front of a mirror and, catching a glimpse of something in his own reflection, would think: "Oh, that looks like so-and-so." And the impression would develop from there. The last thing he would do before going onstage was to look into the mirror one last time—not out of vanity but because the mirror gave him comfort, inspiration and self-assurance. Yet he understood that the true magic didn't come from the face in the mirror, or even the voices of unknown origin—ultimately the magic came from empathy, from Jim's uncanny gift for projecting an emotion that summed up the essence of a subject's personality.

Leatrice Spevack went all out to put the essential elements in place to create a breakthrough for Jim. She got in touch with every-one she knew in the media; she got her friends to put the word out that something hot was going on at Yuk-Yuk's; and she made sure there were going to be some talent agents and producers on hand. As it happened, opening night turned out to be the performance that had been booked by a group from a private girls' school. That's how screaming Toronto schoolgirls turned into valuable extras on Jim's big night. As one awestruck observer whispered to Leatrice after the show: "It was like seeing the Beatles."

Jim rose to the occasion. He captivated the audience by playing all the characters from the TV sitcom *My Three Sons*. He did a great takeoff on the Amazing Kreskin (an odd talk-show celebrity who claimed to have psychic powers). He brought the house down as Sammy Davis performing the number *Mr. Bojangles* in Las Vegas. And he topped himself with his singing duets—doing both Kermit the Frog and Miss Piggy in one song, both Sonny and Cher in another.

The payoff was beyond what even Leatrice had hoped for. The *Toronto Star,* Canada's largest-circulation newspaper, ran a big photograph of Jim doing his Sammy Davis impression. The headline read: "Up, up goes a new comic star." *Star* critic Bruce Blackadar began his review this way: "It's been a long time—oh, Lord, how long, how LONG!—since I've seen the special type of frantic magic in this town that equaled what happened at Yuk-Yuk's Komedy Kabaret last night. I saw a genuine star coming to life, and that happens so rarely that it's worth shouting out the news to the world. Jim Carrey—here he comes."

Blackadar went on to predict that within five years Carrey would be as renowned as Johnny Carson, Rodney Dangerfield and Richard Pryor. He felt that watching Carrey had been like being present in the early days of Woody Allen's appearances in Greenwich Village. According to Blackadar, Carrey had such intuitive body language, such an acute ear, such manic power that it bordered on genius. And he reported that he had never heard a crowd laugh and cheer as exuberantly as the packed house at Yuk-Yuk's.

That rave notice was just what Jim and Leatrice had been hoping for, and it changed everything. Even Mark Breslin was impressed. He made the shrewd decision to cancel the comedian he had booked as the featured act for the following week and instead hold Carrey over for a second week. Suddenly everyone wanted to book Jim Carrey. And the mood was so ebullient that Jim and Leatrice danced in the street.

They knew they had won some kind of jackpot, and every day there was fresh proof. In response to Blackadar's review, other newspapers wanted articles about Jim. Within a week his standard fee for an appearance had gone up from $100 a night to $1,000 a night. This meant that Leatrice's boss, Demi Thompson, would no longer be dismayed that she was spending so much time promoting a guy who brought in only $15 in commissions for each appearance. It also meant that the Carrey family could afford to live in the city instead of at Jackson's Point. They moved into a basement apartment on Walmer Road just north of Bloor Street. And as a result of the publicity, Jim was signed by an agent who booked actors for radio and television commercials. He was soon being invited to appear as a guest on local radio and TV talk shows, which gave him a chance to reach a wider public than those who hung out at comedy clubs.

Around this time, Jim was cast in *Introducing Janet*, a dramatic film being made in Toronto for CBC-TV. Ironically, he made his screen debut in the role of a young man named Tony who aspires to be a comedian but is not very good at it. Produced and directed by Glen Salzman and Rebecca Yates, *Introducing Janet* was conceived as a half-hour film aimed at teenagers and scheduled for a late-afternoon (after-school) time slot. Nada Harcourt, the CBC executive then in charge of children's programming, was so enthusiastic that the film was expanded to fill an hour.

Salzman caught Carrey's act while he was researching the comedy scene. He was looking for background details, not scouting performers, but Salzman was so taken with Carrey that he returned the next night with Yates, at that time his wife and business partner. They decided to audition Jim, and they were impressed by his dramatic ability. It was obvious Jim had talent that went beyond stand-up comedy.

Janet, played by Adah Glassbourg (whose brother Michael Glassbourg wrote the script), has a pushy mother, is fat and suffers from low self-esteem. Carrey played Janet's friend Tony, a waiter and aspiring comedian at a club called Giggles (though actually the club scenes were shot at Yuk-Yuk's). Tony is not nearly as talented or accomplished as he would like to be, and Janet gains confidence by helping Tony improve his act. In one scene, she shows him how to do a Groucho Marx impression. But when Tony gets laryngitis before the big night, she finds herself on the spot: she has to go on in his place. And not being a comedian, she has no material to fall back on except telling the truth about herself.

It would be an understatement to say that this venture did not give Jim a chance to showcase his talents as a comedian. In fact, the film put Jim into the odd position of having to perform deliberately bad material—including a really dreadful routine in which Tony does an amateurish impression of the Fonz from *Happy Days* doing a cooking show. Carrey was taking a big risk, because the more convincing he was in the role, the more viewers might find it hard to believe that the real Jim Carrey had talent.

In an interview with *TV Guide*, Carrey tried to emphasize the difference between the performing styles of Jim and Tony: "It's totally different, because I never rely on someone else to help, either in writing or performing." But he admitted that doing Tony's bad impression of the Fonz was an unsettling experience. "Isn't that horrible? They wrote that. I wouldn't write something like that. It's ghastly."

Still, Carrey insisted he was grateful to have a chance to prove himself as an actor who could get a part across as written. Though *Introducing Janet* did not generate too much excitement when it was shown on the CBC in September 1981, it achieved a surprising afterlife on video thanks to Carrey's later fame, and it is still in circulation under a title that stresses his participation: *Rubber Face*.

0   0   0

IN THE SPRING of 1981, Leatrice Spevack was finding that the more momentum she managed to achieve for Jim's career, the more pressure she was under to accelerate his rise to the top. A lot of the pressure was coming from Percy. But it was becoming clear that getting great press in Toronto could take a performer only so far, and it wouldn't make you a star in the United States.

For this reason, in the last week of June, Leatrice took Jim to New York for a crack at the big time. She knew the competition was cutthroat, with thousands of New York comics vying for five-minute spots at well-known comedy clubs in hopes that they might catch the attention of producers and talent scouts. Leatrice sent out promotional packages, used her contacts at the clubs (where she used to scout acts for Yuk-Yuk's) and called in as many favors as she could. Her trump card was the video made from Jim's recent triumph at Yuk-Yuk's.

The entourage that made the trip from Toronto included not only Jim and Leatrice but also Avi Koren, Jim's sound man and sidekick, and Dennis Kucherawy, an entertainment reporter who hoped to write a magazine article about Jim's New York debut. They all stayed at the Algonquin Hotel, and it wasn't cheap. Because Jim would not be paid for his appearances at comedy club showcases, Leatrice was hoping that she could find a paying gig to offset the cost of the trip. She managed to do so with a booking at Dangerfield's, the club owned by comedian Rodney Dangerfield. To get clearance from U.S. Immigration authorities to work in New York, they had claimed that Jim was doing an audition.

On their first night in New York, a wide-eyed Jim took a walk along Broadway with Avi and Dennis. He wanted to see the CBS theater where Ed Sullivan had introduced the Beatles to North

America. And at about 2:00 a.m. they went past the apartment building on the Upper West Side known as the Dakota, where only months earlier John Lennon had been assassinated. They talked to other young Lennon fans who had made the same pilgrimage, and on the spot Jim began doing an impression of Lennon, singing *Imagine*. In Kucherawy's memory, it stands out as a poignant moment.

Onstage, Jim found New York audiences a bit chilly. They had a taste for smart-ass social commentators (which Jim wasn't), and they didn't know quite what to make of a guy who seemed to have wandered in by mistake from Las Vegas. At Catch a Rising Star he waited and waited and waited for a chance to go on, and then had the misfortune to be given a spot immediately after a then-unknown woman named Sandra Bernhard. Her malevolent stream-of-consciousness act was a decided downer that left the audience in a foul mood. The diehard customers who bothered to stick around were in no mood for some hick from Canada who sang like Kermit the Frog. At first, Carrey got no response from the audience, and the management flashed a light indicating that he was supposed to get off the stage. But according to Kucherawy, "Jim ignored the flashing light, stayed on and won the crowd over. He said afterward he was determined not to pay the price for what the previous act had done."

As Leatrice remembers, Jim charmed the crowd at the Comic Strip, but the manager wasn't terribly interested in him. He was too busy cultivating a young comedian who was appearing regularly at the club but wasn't yet well known: Eddie Murphy.

It was at the Improvisation that Leatrice heard Jim Carrey's prospects accurately summed up. The club was run by Silver Friedman (ex-wife of *Improv* founder Budd Friedman), who welcomed the Canadian visitor with an eight-minute spot. Jim did a stunning set, and the audience was wild for it. Surveying the scene from the back of the club, a veteran comedian known as Uncle Dirty grinned at Leatrice and quipped: "He's not Lenny, but he's money."

That week, the only money was coming from Dangerfield's. That was the main reason for playing there, because as far as Leatrice was concerned, Dangerfield's was a tourist trap. The response of the audience at Dangerfield's was polite but hardly delirious, and Jim's magic seemed not to be working—until the night Rodney himself showed up and immediately took a shine to Jim. This encounter would do more to advance Jim's career than anything else that happened in New York that week. As a result, Carrey would make several return trips to New York for week-long engagements at Dangerfield's. He would become a personal favorite of Rodney, and would frequently be hired as the opening act when Dangerfield was doing a show in Canada.

0 0 0

bACK IN Toronto, Leatrice had the idea that, since Jim's career was going so well, she could leave Square Sun Productions and, taking Jim with her, set up an independent company. It didn't occur to her to question Jim's loyalty to her, even though they had never had any contract except a handshake. When she told her boss Demi Thompson about this plan, Demi asked her to stay and offered to improve her deal. She could spend as much time as she liked on Jim's career, she would get a raise, she could even own a piece of Square Sun. She accepted the offer.

But a few months later it became clear that she was being squeezed out. Revenue from bar bands had dwindled, and the company was heavily in debt. Demi called Leatrice in and told her that she would have to handle more bands, and he would take over Jim's management. He had been getting closely involved with Jim and Percy, and he claimed that they wanted him in charge.

In fact there had long been an awkward and unspoken conflict between Leatrice and Percy. She would never have said this out loud to anyone at the time, but she felt Percy wanted to live his life through Jim. "I thought it was wrong of Jim's parents to put so much of a burden on him," she says now. "I just didn't think it was fair to do that to someone so young."

The unspoken animosity was mutual. Percy felt more comfortable with Demi, and he told Demi about his lack of confidence in Leatrice. Faced with this power play, Leatrice had little choice but to quit. At first she naively assumed that Jim would leave Square Sun with her, and she was devastated when she learned he had chosen to stay with Demi. In any case, the old company was about to be disbanded. Demi was taking on a partner, Ron Scribner, and they would set up their new office atop a spot on Eglinton Avenue that Scribner owned, called Café on the Park.

Leatrice felt outraged and betrayed, but she knew also that she was playing a losing hand in the oldest showbiz game in the world, the one in which a manager builds a fresh talent into a rising star and then gets shunted aside. She was not going to go quietly. Her emotional confrontation with Jim Carrey took place at W.C. Fields restaurant, only a block from Yuk-Yuk's.

Jim brought Wayne Flemming for moral support. Leatrice prepared a list of all the things she had achieved for Jim, all the deals she had arranged. She didn't want him to harbor any illusions that Demi deserved the credit for the work she had done on her client's behalf. Leatrice also had the satisfaction of telling Jim that he was making a big mistake, and of predicting that Demi would not be able to deliver what Jim wanted.

Leatrice and Jim had never become close personal friends, not just because she was older, but because they came from different worlds and didn't have much in common beyond their mutual interest in Jim's career. Some observers who saw them constantly together, sometimes even sharing hotel rooms, wondered whether their relationship might turn into a romance, but the possibility never occurred to either of them. Jim realized he had come a long way with Leatrice and shared some great moments with her. This final meeting, however, was decidedly not one of them.

Hearing Leatrice's parting shots, Jim felt overwhelmed and disturbed both by the information she was delivering and by the intensity of her pain and outrage. He was not yet twenty years old, and he liked to think of himself as a generous and decent human being, not as a ruthless manipulator. Indeed, Jim was so shaken by this confrontation that he had to make a run for the basement washroom to throw up. The business of comedy, it had become clear to both parties in this disintegrating relationship, was not always a laughing matter.

ON tHE rOAD

tHE BONDING of Demi Thompson and Jim Carrey happened in the fall of 1981, when Demi, rather than Leatrice Spevack, accompanied Jim on an exciting and important trip to Los Angeles. A talent coordinator for Budd Friedman's comedy club the Improvisation (which by then had an L.A. branch as well as the original New York location) had visited Toronto, seen Jim perform and booked him to appear in L.A. The club had a high profile through the cable TV show produced there, *An Evening at the Improv*. Leatrice organized the trip.

For Jim, who had made an unsuccessful trip to L.A. more than a year earlier (he'd auditioned for a chance to appear at the Comedy Store and been turned down), this was an opportunity he had dreamed of. It would give him a chance to be discovered, at age nineteen, by the kind of powerful Hollywood people who could cast him in a movie or a TV show. But before making the trip, Jim had to wait for official papers from the United States Department of Immigration giving him permission to work temporarily in the

U.S., and there were a lot of frustrating delays to be endured and bits of red tape to be untangled before the day arrived when he could board the plane.

After the flight from Toronto, Jim and Demi checked into the Hyatt on Sunset (next door to the Comedy Store) in West Hollywood, where they were sharing a room, then decided to go to a movie. Walking down Sunset Boulevard, they came to Mann's Chinese Theater, where Jim wanted to take a close look at the names of the stars set in cement. He told Demi matter-of-factly that one day his own name would be there. According to Thompson, this wasn't a fantasy or an expression of ego. It was just a matter of fact; Jim had complete confidence it would happen.

They decided to see a movie that had just opened, *On Golden Pond*. It would turn out to be the source of one of Jim's most memorable routines. Even while the film was running, Jim was trying to learn how to mimic both Katharine Hepburn and Henry Fonda. And when the movie ended, and Demi was ready to head back to the hotel, Jim insisted on sitting through it again. By the time they got back to the Hyatt, it was 3:00 a.m. in L.A. (6:00 a.m. Toronto time) and they had been up for twenty-four hours.

The next day, Demi awoke to find Jim at the foot of his bed trying out his Katharine Hepburn impression. It was more than Demi could take. "Jim," he pleaded, "could you please speak to me in your own voice?"

When Jim did his act at the Improv, there was a fairly full house, including not just regular customers but a smattering of show-business people—agents and producers scouting new talent. One of them was Bud Robinson, a friend of club owner Budd Friedman. Robinson managed several comedians, including an up-and-coming one named Johnny Dark, and he also handled Doc

Severinsen, leader of the Tonight Show Band. Robinson had been a performer himself, with a long career in vaudeville; he and his wife had once done an act as a dance team. And his list of friends included Lucille Ball, Johnny Carson, Ed McMahon and Ruth Buzzi (the veteran comedian best remembered for her TV breakthrough on *Laugh-In*).

Robinson was favorably impressed with Jim's act, and the next day, Budd Friedman passed a message to Demi to call his office. Though he wasn't prepared to get professionally involved in handling Carrey, Robinson offered to do anything he could to help Jim get discovered in L.A.

Robinson arranged for Demi and Jim to meet Ruth Buzzi, and they were invited to go to Burbank and meet several people at *The Tonight Show*. Among them were Johnny Carson, Ed McMahon and the show's talent coordinator, Jim McCauley. There was a lot of positive talk about having Jim appear on the show, and a tentative date was proposed. But the next step was that Jim would have to plan another appearance at the Improv in early 1982 so that McCauley could see his act.

Back in Toronto, Jim was working steadily and winning new fans. On New Year's Eve, he appeared at the glitzy Imperial Room of the Royal York Hotel in a variety show that was carried on CBC-TV. Wearing a blue suit with a red tie and blue sunglasses, Carrey teased the audience: "You look like a cultured, intelligent group—and also very gullible." Then he asked the crowd for a blood-curdling scream "to release all your anger from 1981." Among the impressions he performed that night were Tom Jones, swiveling his hips, and Sammy Davis Jr. appearing at Caesar's Palace in Las Vegas singing *Mr. Bojangles*. But the high point of Carrey's act on this occasion was a touching impression, infused with affection, of

Billie Holiday, wearing a white gardenia in her hair. It topped the portrayal of Holiday by Diana Ross in the movie bio *Lady Sings the Blues*.

Jim was so excited about his date with Johnny Carson that he prematurely let the word get around, and reports began appearing in Toronto newspapers that Jim had been invited to be a guest on *The Tonight Show*. He could hardly wait to get back to Los Angeles. But when he and Demi returned to the Improv in February, they suddenly felt a big chill coming from Burbank. The morning after Jim's appearance at the club, he and Demi got the worst call they had ever received. Jim's act had not gone over well with Johnny Carson's talent co-ordinator. McCauley felt Jim wasn't suitable to appear on the show at that time. He needed to polish his act first.

According to Thompson, the problem was the patter linking Jim's impressions of Johnny Mathis, Kermit the Frog, Mick Jagger, Popeye and so on. To be sure of getting laughs, Jim peppered his act with raunchy jokes. In one sketch he had Ronald Reagan (then a recent arrival in the White House) talking to Nancy over the intercom while she was in bed with General Alexander Haig. And in his *Star Wars* bit, Jim portrayed Darth Vader making an obscene phone call to Yoda. All this was fairly tame by the anything-goes standards of comedy clubs, but it was problematic for NBC. Unfortunately, the blue material was intrinsic to the act; it couldn't be easily edited out without having the whole routine unravel.

Jim was not only crushed by the rejection but embarrassed about the fact that he had let the word out—his anticipated debut on *The Tonight Show* was now public knowledge in Toronto. When he got back home, journalists kept asking about it. Feeling it would be too damaging and humiliating to have the real story told in the press, Jim decided to do a bit of spin-doctoring. Consequently, the *Toronto Star* ran a huge article across the top of the front page of its entertainment section on April 2 with the headline: "The man who said no to Johnny Carson." A subheadline amplified: "But Canada's hot impressionist wasn't being rude. He says he just wasn't ready."

According to the article, written by Rob Salem, Carrey dropped down to the *Star* to explain why he'd backed out of his date with Carson. "It was all set," he told Salem, "but at the last minute we decided to pull out. We figured I'm better off not to do it right now, especially since they said I can come back anytime. So many doors fly open if it goes well on the Carson show, and if you're not ready to go through those doors there's not much point taking the chance."

Luckily, Jim didn't have time to go into a funk about this set-back. He was getting a lot of bookings, both in Toronto and on the road. And whenever he wasn't otherwise engaged, he would do a week at the Café on the Park, owned by Demi's partner Ron Scribner. A lot of well-known musical acts were appearing there (the café had a cover charge and offered a dinner-show package). The place became a kind of hangout for insiders, and Jim would often turn up on nights when he wasn't working. Carrey continued to earn a lot of attention from the Toronto media. He was a frequent guest on local radio and TV shows and often the subject of feature articles in the newspapers. And celebrities would sometimes drop by to see the young impressionist, among them Robin Williams, Catherine O'Hara and Rodney Dangerfield.

By mid-1982, Ron Scribner had hired Percy Carrey as a part-time bookkeeper, working three days a week. Percy, eager to keep up with Jim's career, sometimes answered the office phone; if there was a call for Demi that sounded as if it might be about Jim, Percy would put it through to Demi, then pop into his office as soon as he was off the phone to see what was going on.

Within the industry, the buzz about Jim was spreading, and a lot of offers were coming in. For a while, Jim Carrey became a top choice of touring celebrities to open a show. Carrey opened for Ian Tyson at the Imperial Room and for Andy Williams at the vast Ontario Place Forum. Williams seemed a little tired, according to one reviewer, but the crowd of seven thousand gave a warm ovation to Jim after he performed his own charming and touching version of *On Golden Pond*.

Rodney Dangerfield, a veteran comedy performer of the old school, not only hired him to open shows when he was appearing in Canada but also invited his protégé to tour with him and appear for a week at Caesar's Palace in Las Vegas. Percy tagged along for part of the time and developed a jocular rapport with Dangerfield. And Rodney became another father figure to Jim, not only giving him tips on the business but also announcing over dinner (perhaps flippantly) that it was really time for Jim to settle down and get married.

In mid-April, Jim and Demi flew to Colorado for something completely different. Jim had won a leading role in a lightweight made-for-TV movie about a Club Med ski resort, *Copper Mountain*. The movie was produced by Damien Lee, a former ski racer who had been producing sports telecasts for the CTV network. With the participation of his friend Moses Znaimer, the shrewd and flamboyant owner of Toronto's feisty Citytv, and the deep pockets of the new pay-TV franchise First Choice, Lee produced the film on a phenomenally low budget of $125,000. He and writer-director David Mitchell came up with a story that combined great scenery, sports action, pop music and a hint of sex. The resort was available on the cheap for a one-week shoot, because the ski season was just about over. Lee got the resort to provide rooms and facilities free in exchange for the promotional value of the film. Carrey's fee for appearing in the film was $7,500.

The sketchy script is merely an excuse to put some musicians—including vocalist Rita Coolidge and Toronto rock-and-roll veteran Rompin' Ronnie Hawkins—in an outdoor setting against the mountains and toss in some pretty women. Carrey plays a rather charming young fellow named Bob who is shyly on the make, but in need of some mentoring by his older and wiser friend, played by Alan Thicke. And it just so happens that Bob is a kid from Ontario who, as he confides at one point, gets nervous around women, so he starts doing celebrity impressions. It's a way of hiding; he's afraid to be himself. And the impressions keep scaring the women away. Carrey had little experience with skiing, but according to David Mitchell, he was willing to try anything and was not discouraged by a few tumbles.

This is not a movie anyone would make the mistake of taking seriously. "*Copper Mountain* was so terrible not even Jim was funny," Alan Thicke remarked afterward. It's certainly slapdash, but it's also amusing in a certain empty-headed way, and it does provide a wonderful snapshot of the young Jim Carrey—of what he was like before he became a polished Hollywood performer—which is helpful to anyone trying to understand where Jim Carrey came from.

Despite thirteen hours of filming every day, the cast and crew did their best to have a good time. One night, Jim put on an hour-long show to entertain the others, and he had some of his cohorts crying with laughter. According to Danny Marks, a guitar player who was backing Hawkins and Coolidge, "Jim was the funniest guy

I've ever been in the presence of. He was warm, and everyone liked him. He had so much energy we all wondered if he ever slept. And we all knew he would go on to do great things."

The blond ingenue in the movie is Ziggy Lorenc, who went on to become a popular on-camera figure at Citytv but was at the time a twenty-four-year-old aspiring actress working on the station's switchboard. Jim and Ziggy spent much of the week flirting. In her memoir *Life on Venus Ave.*, Lorenc recalls that Jim followed her around like a little puppy. "He's so cute," she wrote, using the present tense, diary style. "He reminds me of a farm boy. Not only is he talented, he's young and confident and happy and his spirit is unbroken."

Jim and Ziggy went dancing at the resort's disco and enjoyed a goodnight kiss, but then Ziggy's boyfriend flew in, and the romance was put on hold. But there was unquestionably a spark, and the two were destined to reconnect a few months later.

Around this time, Richard Crouse, then breaking into journalism while working at the bar of the restaurant Mr. Greenjeans in Toronto's Eaton Centre, spotted a guy sitting alone at the bar who had apparently been stood up by a girl. "You look a lot like Jim Carrey," he said. "I am Jim Carrey," replied the man at the bar. The two became friends, and Carrey would often put Crouse on the guest list for his shows at the Café on the Park. Crouse taped an interview with Carrey.

"Movies are all right, but there's a lot of waiting around when you're making them," Carrey told Crouse. "It's boring. I have to be going all the time. Go, go, go. I get so anxious when I have to wait. Onstage is where I get my kicks. Being live onstage is the best feeling in the world."

Carrey was already living part of the time in Los Angeles,

traveling back and forth frequently. Ron Scribner had helped find him a place to live, sharing a house in West Hollywood with a couple of other guys who aspired to careers in show business, including songwriter Phil Roy. When in L.A., Jim was taking acting classes from a man named Vincent Chasen, who had coached Tom Selleck and many of the performers on *Saturday Night Live*.

Back in Toronto, Jim and Ron Scribner had a serious talk while drinking kahlua one night after closing time at the Café on the Park. Ron was a reader of self-help books, and he had been especially influenced by Dale Carnegie and Norman Vincent Peale. Ron believed in setting goals—such as becoming internationally renowned or earning more than $100,000 a year—and he shared his philosophy with Jim, who seemed to like the idea. In fact, that's where he got the notion—which would later become part of his legend—of writing himself a postdated check for $10 million.

Scribner spent some time on the road with Jim. Once they went to Pittsburgh for a gig at a comedy club. Another time they were driving from Grand Island, New York, where Jim had performed, to Saratoga Springs, where Jim was supposed to open a show for Andy Williams. As they drove along the highway, Jim cranked up the rock-and-roll on the car radio and sang along. But his mood changed when they reached Saratoga Springs and realized they had left the cassette tapes with prerecorded music for Jim's act back in Grand Island. A frantic phone call brought the news that the tapes had been found on the sidewalk at the hotel next to the spot where they had parked their car. After a talk with the management for Andy Williams, Jim opted not to perform at all.

As 1982 went by, Jim became more and more eager to make a permanent move to L.A. He wanted either Demi or Ron to go with him, but they said they had to stay in Toronto to make a living.

But Jim was absolutely determined, and one day that fall, he happened to run into the one person who seemed capable of making it possible: David Holiff.

Carrey and Holiff had met at Yuk-Yuk's in 1979. At that time, Holiff had been an assistant manager of the club, but he had other aspirations. While still working at Yuk-Yuk's, he began booking gigs for Howie Mandel and a few other comics, which inevitably led to a parting of the ways with Mark Breslin. In fact it was Holiff who booked Carrey into the Montreal club Stitches in 1980, infuriating Mark Breslin. Holiff not only became Mandel's manager, he took him to Los Angeles, where Holiff relentlessly promoted Mandel until he landed a continuing role on the successful ABC television series *St. Elsewhere*. But shortly afterward, Mandel and Holiff parted company.

Holiff had recently returned to Toronto when Carrey ran into him. Holiff was still smarting from Mandel's defection, and he was at loose ends. His chance encounter with Carrey had an air of predestination about it. At this particular moment in their lives, Jim Carrey and David Holiff seemed to be made for each other.

AT tHE COMEDY STORE

fOR YEARS, the mere mention of David Holiff's name would cause some comedy insiders to murmur: "*Broadway Danny Rose*." They were alluding to one of Woody Allen's darkest showbiz satires, in which a hyperactive theatrical manager puts his whole life into transforming his clients, unknown comedians, into stars. Then, when one of them makes it big, he tells him: "Hey, Danny, look! We're just not seeing eye to eye any more. I gotta move on." David Holiff even looked and sounded a bit like Danny Rose as played by Woody: aggressively verbal and notably eccentric.

The movie didn't come out until 1984, but by the time he ran into Jim Carrey in the fall of 1982, David Holiff was already living the part of Danny Rose, almost as if he'd read the script in advance. Indeed, he had just gone through the experience of having Howie Mandel deliver the same message that Danny gets, in one of the movie's most memorable scenes, from the guy he has made into a star: "I appreciate all you done. It's just—I don't need you any more."

Holiff was a born hustler, and he had a family history to help him along. His parents, Joy and Morry Holiff, had invented the kind of wallet that holds credit cards and made millions through a company called Ambassador Leather Goods—first in Toronto, then in Niagara Falls and eventually in Phoenix, Arizona. And Saul Holiff, David's uncle, had been country singing star Johnny Cash's manager for thirteen years.

After graduating from college in Arizona in the early 1970s, David headed for L.A. and a hot new club called the Comedy Store on Sunset Boulevard. A 1960s flower child who dressed like a hippie and talked like a salesman, Holiff would spend hours watching comics like Richard Pryor and Rodney Dangerfield. When Holiff moved to Colorado, he opened a natural food restaurant and used some of the profits to book little-known comics, including Robin Williams, to perform there for $100 a week plus expenses.

By the late 1970s, Holiff was back in Toronto, and naturally he was drawn to Yuk-Yuk's. He watched the audience go wild for Howie Mandel, who did nutty sketches about a demented racing driver and a screwball named Crazy Donny. By 1979, Mandel was ready to make a move. At twenty-two, he was already very popular in Toronto but unknown in the United States (exactly as Carrey would be three years later). At this point, Holiff became his manager as well as his booking agent and took him to Los Angeles. Mandel did a few TV shows, he started playing at the Comedy Store, and he secured a green card, allowing him to work and live in the United States.

In Los Angeles, Holiff went into overdrive—badgering gossip columnists, cajoling booking agents, bugging everyone he could think of to come out and take a look at this unknown young comic from Toronto, who, he kept assuring people, was going to make it big. Before long, insiders were talking not only about Howie's act but about David's amazing success in getting media exposure for his client. Here was a guy who wouldn't take no for an answer, who would call people at all hours of the day and night, until people came to see his client's act just to get David off their backs.

The promotion paid off, as journalist Paul King documented in a 1985 article in *Toronto Life* magazine. Howie got parts in several Canadian-produced movies in 1980 and 1981. And then came the big break. Holiff persuaded a casting agent named Molly Lopata to catch Howie's act at the Comedy Store. She loved it, and she happened to be head of casting for the hugely successful television production company MTM. A few months later, Mandel was signed for the continuing role of Dr. Wayne Fiscus in MTM's new series *St. Elsewhere*.

Less than a month later, Howie broke the news to David: he didn't need him any more. Holiff claimed he had a five-year contract with Mandel, and there was a major dispute about money, involving hundreds of thousands of dollars in commissions. The legal battle went on for years and ended with an out-of-court settlement. But for Holiff there was more involved than the money and the legal battle; he felt personally betrayed.

Back in Toronto, David was still feeling let down by this turn of events when he bumped into Jim Carrey. At this point, Jim's greatest wish was to have someone do for him exactly what David had done for Howie: take him to L.A., book gigs for him at the comedy clubs there, get the media to notice him and drag TV and movie producers and casting agents to catch his act.

To a person like Holiff, the prospect of handling Jim Carrey must have been irresistible. Jim was young and sensationally talented, but a completely unknown commodity in L.A., where only a mentor like David would know how to get him the right kind of attention. Still, there were a few reasons to proceed cautiously. First of all, Jim already had representation—Demi Thompson and Ron Scribner—and Holiff knew he couldn't take Jim on unless Carrey had no commitments to other managers.

Jim and David had a series of conversations and meetings, and a plan gradually evolved. Jim had been pressing Demi for a permanent move to L.A., but Demi's response was that it was much too soon, and Jim would starve to death while appearing for next to nothing at the L.A. comedy clubs. As far as Jim was concerned, it was worth the sacrifice. That fall, after talking to Holiff, Jim asked Demi to meet him near the Carrey apartment on Walmer Road. Jim said he knew Demi wasn't prepared to move to L.A. with him, but Jim didn't want to wait any longer, so he was going to make the move with another manager. It was an emotional conversation, but Demi wasn't able to change Jim's mind. They agreed to an amicable parting. Jim then called David to tell him there was no problem with Demi.

Two hurdles remained. Jim was still just twenty, and his parents—especially Percy—were opposed to the move. They didn't understand why Jim couldn't simply stay home and continue going to L.A. on occasional trips when necessary. According to Holiff, it was clear that Jim wanted to break away from Percy, and it was a delicate situation. David had his lawyers draw up a contract. Percy got involved in the negotiations and kept raising objections. It was clear to Holiff that Percy didn't like him and didn't trust him. According to Holiff, Jim said he wanted a three-month trial period instead, after which he would be willing to sign a deal. Holiff's lawyer and his mother both advised him not to agree to such an arrangement. But, faced with the alternatives of losing this opportunity or working without a contract, Holiff decided in the end to take a chance.

In January 1983, Jim and his new manager made the move to L.A. David's connections with the Comedy Store and its legendary owner, Mitzi Shore, quickly began to pay off.

Jim was absolutely right to be excited about being on that stage. It was at the Comedy Store that the two most excitingly talented and original comedians of the preceding decade, Robin Williams and Richard Pryor, had scored career breakthroughs. And Mitzi Shore was the miracle woman who kept the whole carnival going. The club had fallen into her hands as part of her 1973 divorce from Sammy Shore, a stand-up comic who, eighteen months earlier, had turned a small room on the Sunset Strip into a spot where he and his colleagues could get together. It began as a helter-skelter operation where the jokes were free and the drinks cost seventy-five cents each. Comics would hang out, and sometimes were asked to perform while having a drink at the bar. Sammy himself would get up every so often and do a ten-minute routine.

But it was Mitzi, not Sammy, who deserved the credit for turning the club into a thriving business. She bought the building on Sunset, where she operated three different rooms, and eventually she opened a couple of offshoot clubs and organized a touring troupe of comics to perform on the college circuit. Mitzi's timing could not have been better. A few years earlier, when the comedy business was becoming a growth industry, all the action seemed to be in New York, especially at the Improvisation, not far from the Broadway theater district. But just before the Comedy Store opened, Johnny Carson moved *The Tonight Show* from New York to Los Angeles, making L.A. the undisputed capital of TV talk shows. In the mid-1970s, Budd Friedman moved to L.A. and opened a branch of the Improv on Melrose Avenue, but despite the competition, Mitzi remained the queen of L.A.'s comedy scene. The comedians who played her club would mention her name on TV, and before long the Comedy Store had become an institution and a tourist attraction.

Because she alone had the power to decide who would appear, and when, and in which room, Mitzi was powerful and feared. If a TV network wanted to look at ten comedians on a certain evening in search of one to do a guest spot, it was Mitzi who decided which ten would be on the bill. If a certain comic was dying to be seen by a certain producer who was planning to come to the club late Thursday, Mitzi was the one who said yes or no. The comics who performed at the Comedy Store all craved her approval, and when they went out together late at night after all the performances were over, what did they talk about? Mitzi.

In the late 1970s, Mitzi's image took a battering, as Calvin Trillin explained in a lengthy article in *The New Yorker* in 1980. Mitzi found herself at the center of a nasty controversy when the comedians got together and proposed a revolutionary idea: that the performers at the Comedy Store should be paid. To Mitzi it was an outrageous demand: it had always been understood that the point of working at the Comedy Store was not to get money but to have the opportunity to be seen by people who might one day make you very rich. To make an appearance there was to take a gamble; the club was not an employer but a springboard to something else. But the comedians couldn't afford to wait for a future payoff: they needed to eat and pay the rent *now*. And since Mitzi was raking in so much money, she could certainly afford to share the loot with the talent. The dispute could have been resolved with token concessions from Mitzi, but she took a hard line. In 1979, with negotiations going nowhere, the comedians went on strike.

The strike got uglier and uglier and it dragged on for seven weeks before Mitzi finally agreed that the comedians would be paid. An air of bitterness lingered beyond the settlement. In the aftermath, Mitzi was accused of punishing comedians who had been leaders of the strike, and a comedian named Steve Lubetkin committed suicide by jumping off the roof of the hotel next door to the club.

By the time Jim Carrey arrived on the scene, things were pretty much back to normal at the Comedy Store, and Mitzi was back on her throne. In an average week, Mitzi might see one hundred new comics audition, but she immediately spotted Jim as something special. Joey Gaynor, a comedian from Newark who had been appearing at the Comedy Store for several years before Jim arrived, recalls: "Mitzi could be hot and cold with some people, and a lot of us didn't like some of the things she did. But there's no question she did everything she could for Jim. He was always one of Mitzi's favorites."

Debbie Pearl, a writer who was David Holiff's girlfriend at the time, remembers Carrey as one of the good guys—a sweet, charming, big-hearted kid who was always gracious and fun to be with: "He was wildly creative, and often there was some new bit he was developing that he was eager to try out on you. Later it would turn up in his act. I used to wonder what it must be like living inside his skin with all that was going on. Mitzi really loved Jim. If she hadn't, he would not have flourished the way he did."

Before long, Jim was performing several nights a week at the club, and audiences were squealing with delight. They responded positively to the fact that, unlike many of the other performers, he wasn't fat, bald or scruffy. Some people thought it was weird that in L.A., the world capital of open collars, Jim always wore a suit. But as far as he was concerned, it gave him more flexibility; he could impersonate almost anyone, which would not be the case if he were wearing some trendy outfit. Jim's creative energy was amazing. He was constantly improving and adding new material—such as a bit about Gene Kelly dancing the title song from *Singin' in the Rain* while trying to put a dime into a parking meter. The way he could transform himself into James Dean, walking away and gradually assuming Dean's air of sullenness at being misunderstood, made audiences gasp.

When reporters asked Mitzi about Jim, she would say that no one since Robin Williams had been this hot at the Comedy Store. And thanks to David Holiff, hundreds of producers, agents, talent scouts and TV network executives poured in to catch Jim's act. When it came to getting the word out and creating a buzz, David Holiff was without peer. "David had every big name in Hollywood down to see Jim," Debbie recalls. "People were aware Jim was a major talent. The only question was exactly what to do with him."

Jim was as wide-eyed as Dorothy in Oz, savoring every minute of his adventure. When Jim was performing, Mitzi would usually have him go onstage around 9:30. Frequently Jim would stay at the club until midnight when his friend Sam Kinison—known for his rage and dark, edgy style of comedy—would be scheduled. Often, Jim would wind up in the wee hours at Canter's Deli on Fairfax, not far from his house. According to Joey Gaynor, Jim was popular with the other young comics who would hang around at the club and then go out to eat late at night, after the show was over. "Most of us were a little cracked," says Joey Gaynor. "Jimmy fit in because he was one of the guys. He liked to party and have a good time."

He would usually stay up until five o'clock in the morning, then sleep until noon.

Debbie Pearl took on the job of running sound for Jim's act, putting in the music tapes to go with his singing impressions, and she says that even if she made a mistake and there was no sound, Jim never lost his temper. Debbie and Jim had the bond of a shared ambition: they both wanted to be actors, and for a while they took an acting improvisation class together. Where once he seemed content just to keep on doing his impressions on stage, Jim was now hungry for new challenges.

In the meantime, Jim was getting a lot of offers to work in Toronto, but he told David he didn't want to go back. For the first time he felt he had really left home, and he was enjoying the independence. But Jim and David agreed that he would accept a few gigs in Toronto—if there was a lot of money involved. He did take a few offers. One was to do two shows a week at a spot called B.J. Magoon's on Bloor Street West. That same week he became the first Canadian comedian to appear at Roy Thomson Hall, as the opening act for New York comedian Buddy Hackett.

Jim was working at a frantic pace. His schedule included going to Phoenix to appear with Rodney Dangerfield and a quick trip to New York for an appearance at Catch a Rising Star, where network TV executives and the cast of *Saturday Night Live* turned out to have a look at him.

Despite the heavy work schedule and the late-night socializing, Jim was also making time for acting class and many, many hours in front of his mirror, creating new material and improving old material. He concocted a trio of Frank Sinatra, Andy Williams and Charles Aznavour that was a hit with audiences. Other performers might have done individual impressions of these singers; what made Jim's version so much fun was the virtuosity of doing all of them at once, and of playing with the notion of how these rivals would react onstage with one another.

Every so often, Holiff would press for a written contract, but Jim preferred to keep things as they were. Meanwhile, Jim was continuing to score breakthroughs. He was chosen to be featured, along with Robin Williams and Richard Pryor, in a TV special celebrating the Comedy Store's tenth anniversary. And, thanks to Holiff, he acquired both a prestigious Hollywood agent and a well-known publicist to complement Holiff's own efforts as manager.

Debbie Pearl had a connection with Linda Ronstadt (Pearl's best friend was one of Ronstadt's backup singers). One night, Ronstadt came to the Comedy Store to see Jim's act and followed up by having coffee with Jim and David at the hotel next door. Jim was subsequently booked to be the opening act for Ronstadt's forthcoming tour.

But the big thing Jim and David were waiting for was the right TV breakthrough. This was pilot season, and a lot of people had Jim on their shortlists. Executives at ABC had offered a development deal, which would have tied Jim to the network with no guarantee that any project he worked on would actually reach the air. But Jim and David didn't want to be tied up that way. There were auditions for various pilots, including one called *Boone*. It was a part of local mythology that after being spotted at the Comedy Store, Robin Williams won the role of Mork in *Mork and Mindy*, which launched his career. That was the kind of breakthrough Jim and David were looking for. They thought they had found it when Allan Burns came along with *The Duck Factory*.

qUACK, qUACK

IN THE SPRING of 1983, Allan Burns—one of the most respected writer/producers in television—was developing a new series called *The Duck Factory*. After more than a decade at CBS, where he had scored one triumph after another, Burns was producing the new show for NBC, which had been running last among the three big networks and was in need of the kind of boost that shows created by Burns had given CBS. Most new TV shows have the odds stacked against them, but expectations for this one were high, because Burns seemed immune to failure.

After being the co-creator of the phenomenally successful *Smothers Brothers Comedy Hour* in the 1960s, Burns had gone on to win his first Emmy award as the writer for *He and She*, then written several episodes of *Get Smart*. What raised his status from successful to legendary was *The Mary Tyler Moore Show*, which Burns and his collaborator James L. Brooks created for MTM Productions in 1970. The show was not only an instant hit but stayed on the air until 1977; its record has never been matched. Besides being the most popular show on the air, *The Mary Tyler Moore Show* was regarded by many critics as the best comedy series in TV history, winning a phenomenal twenty-nine Emmys in the course of its run.

On the wings of the show's success, MTM Productions became one of the most powerful companies in Hollywood. Burns and Brooks had a long, rewarding association with MTM and its chief executive, Grant Tinker (Mary Tyler Moore's husband). Using characters from *The Mary Tyler Moore Show*, they launched two more successful series: *Rhoda* (with Valerie Harper) and *Lou Grant*. Daringly, the latter was not another half-hour sitcom but a groundbreaking hour-long drama series set in a big-city newsroom. In the title role, Ed Asner came into his own after years of playing the heroine's grumpy but lovable boss on *The Mary Tyler Moore Show*. But Asner was more than the star of the show; he was also president of the Screen Actors Guild and an outspoken activist. And when *Lou Grant* was yanked off the air in 1982 after five seasons, it wasn't the ratings that motivated CBS, if one can believe the rumors, but the desire to avoid the sort of political controversy that Asner provoked.

It was easy to understand why Allan Burns might prefer not to continue his association with CBS. Grant Tinker, who had left MTM to become chairman of floundering NBC, wanted Burns to create a new series, and Burns came up with a concept drawing on his own early years in television. As a young man, Burns had broken into the business working in animation. His boss was an eccentric producer named Jay Ward, who ran a small animation company from cramped headquarters on the Sunset Strip in West Hollywood, across the street from the Chateau Marmont hotel. Ward was known for creating such cartoons as *Rocky and His Friends* and *George of the Jungle*. Burns worked for Ward as a cartoonist from 1961 to

1963. From cartooning, he went on to work on commercials, and to design characters and develop scripts—all for Ward's company. Eventually, Burns and his first partner, Chris Hayward, left Ward's company and broke into more conventional branches of television.

"Everyone in show business is weird," says Burns, who lives in the upscale Brentwood neighborhood of Los Angeles, "but animation people are the weirdest of the weird. Most of them are people stunted in their adolescence. I was a kid from Honolulu in my twenties, and I was intrigued to meet these animators in their fifties and sixties who were so childlike. They had never grown up, and that's what made them fascinating to me. Jay Ward barely paid them a living wage."

Tinker sent Burns to Brandon Tartikoff, the wunderkind who in 1980, at age thirty had become president of the network. Tartikoff would eventually transform NBC into TV's ratings leader with such hit shows as *Cheers*, *Family Ties*, *Golden Girls* and *Miami Vice*. He loved the idea of *Duck Factory*, so Burns wrote scripts for the first two episodes. Tartikoff was extremely enthusiastic about the scripts; he not only wanted the show, he wanted it in a hurry.

Burns started to assemble his ensemble cast, and he was extremely happy with the comedy actors he was able to find for most of the roles. That marvelous veteran Jack Gilford had agreed to play the alcoholic director Brooks Carmichael, while Jay Tarses would play the company's gag-writer, Marty Fenneman. Don Messick was cast as Wally Wooster, a voice-over man who could do six hundred different voices. And Teresa Ganzel would play Sheree Winkler, an airhead from Las Vegas who had married Buddy Winkler, owner of the animation studio, just weeks before his death—and was now taking over his tiny, eccentric empire.

There was just one problem. Burns was baffled when it came to finding someone to play the lead, Skip Tarkenton. Based on Burns himself, Skip was a talented, wide-eyed twenty-two-year-old cartoonist from the American Midwest, moving to Los Angeles to start a new job. Almost as soon as he arrives by bus, he learns that the oddball owner of the animation studio who hired him has suddenly died, and on what is supposed to be Skip's first day at work, his colleagues are arranging the funeral. Nevertheless, Skip stays on and becomes part of the animation factory, which turns out to be a kind of substitute family for him; and he works on a cartoon show (constantly on the verge of being canceled) called *The Dippy Duck Show*.

"For the life of me, I couldn't find the right guy to play Skip," Burns recalls. "I needed someone with a young Jimmy Stewart quality—a sweet guy with a goofy side. One day I had a call from an agent by the name of Jerry Zeitman who had read the script. He said he knew I was having a hard time casting this role, and he knew someone who would be perfect for the part. At first I assumed he was promoting one of his clients, but he was not. He said, 'You've got to get over to the Comedy Store and see this kid Jim Carrey. He is just what you're looking for.'"

Burns went to the Comedy Store and knew within minutes of Carrey starting his act that he had found his Skip Tarkenton: "It was just phenomenal. It was astonishing the way he contorted his body into all kinds of shapes, the way he could do the stances of famous people. I was amazed that a twenty-one-year-old kid could turn around and look exactly like Brezhnev. I was bowled over, but I thought, 'This is a stand-up act of short impressions. How do we know whether he can act?' But then at the end of his performance, Carrey did a five-minute homage to Henry Fonda and

Katharine Hepburn in *On Golden Pond*. It was not only hilarious and stunningly accurate but really very touching. And I thought: 'This is an actor.'"

A few days later, Burns returned to the Comedy Store to see Carrey again. This time he brought Brandon Tartikoff and some of the other top executives from NBC, including Jeff Saganasky. "All of them had the same reaction I did. I remember as we were leaving, Brandon said to me: 'That's your guy. He's terrific.'"

Carrey was offered the part at a salary of $5,000 per episode for the first thirteen episodes with an option to extend the contract if the series were renewed. As far as he and David Holiff were concerned, this was the big break they had been waiting for—a leading role in a TV series being created by the top names in the business. They might not have realized it, but Jim, as the only novice, was the worst-paid member of the cast. Still, by Jim's standards, this was big money. And there was another reason he was eager to do this TV series: it represented a striking departure from the stage act he had been developing for the preceding four years, and he was ready for a change. Jim was starting to see there was a downside to his stage act, and to dread where this career path was taking him. He was getting tired of doing impressions, and he didn't want to wind up in the world capital of impressionist acts, Las Vegas.

The Duck Factory was planned as a mid-season replacement series, meaning that it would not be one of the new shows in NBC's fall lineup in 1983 but would be available to be slotted in once one of the fall shows was identified as a flop. Production was scheduled to begin in Studio City in the fourth week of September.

Instead of resting up before this big career change, Jim spent the most hectic summer of his life. He flew to Phoenix to be the opening act for Rodney Dangerfield; he went on an exhausting thirteen-city tour opening for the Scottish singer Sheena Easton; and he was also doing the concert circuit with Linda Ronstadt. Besides all that, Jim was still appearing at the Comedy Store and doing occasional TV gigs, such as a guest shot on the CTV series *Circus*. His energy level was amazing, and he rarely backed out of a commitment.

In early September Jim flew to Calgary to play a supporting role in a movie directed by the British filmmaker Richard Lester, who had achieved fame in the 1960s as the mastermind of the Beatles' *A Hard Day's Night* and *Help*. *The Next to Last Train Ride* was based on a book by Charles Dennis. By the time the movie was released the following May it was being called *Finders Keepers*, but it would have taken more than a change of title to make it a hit.

Before returning to Los Angeles to start shooting *The Duck Factory*, Jim flew to Toronto to tape an appearance on *Scandals*, a late-night comedy pilot for cable TV, and to be the headliner at an annual luncheon of the Variety Club (a Toronto show-business charity organization) during the Toronto International Film Festival.

During this period, Jim not only had an exhausting work schedule but a rather complicated love life, involving several long-distance relationships. He had started dating Ziggy Lorenc, his *Copper Mountain* co-star, who was still working at Toronto's Citytv on the switchboard. Her boss, Moses Znaimer, invited her to see Jim at the Imperial Room of the Royal York, and Ziggy was charmed when Jim told her the reason he wanted to date her was that she looked like a gangster's main squeeze. When Jim was in town, he and Ziggy would hang out together at Wayne

Flemming's apartment in Scarborough. One day he dropped in to visit her at the TV studio during a call-in contest the station was running. Ziggy's task was to thank scores of people calling in and inform them that a winner had already been chosen. Jim began picking up the phone lines, and startled callers could have sworn they heard Sammy Davis Jr., Jack Nicholson or Katharine Hepburn deliver the disappointing news that they were not contest winners.

Jim had also become involved that year with a Toronto showbusiness publicist seven years his senior who had met him the previous May when he was booked to entertain Canadian cable TV executives at a conference in Calgary. After the show, the publicist joined Jim, David Holiff and another woman who had been working at the conference on a larky car trip to Banff. In the car Jim entertained the others by singing *Every Breath You Take*, a hit song for The Police. And Jim was so funny that his companions were all in stitches as they climbed up and down mountains.

The publicist recalls being completely smitten. "I just had to have him," she says. She and Jim spent three nights together in Banff, and she was amazed that a kid of twenty-one could turn out to be such a skilled and experienced lover. The affair continued off and on for months, sometimes when Jim was in Toronto and other times when the publicist went to L.A. on business. She had an expense account and would take Jim to dinner at top restaurants such as the Ivy. On at least one occasion they wound up having sex in her car in a Santa Monica parking lot. One of the reasons he appreciated her was that she was a great audience—as far as she was concerned, everything he said and did was hilarious. With Jim, she explained happily, you would go to bed laughing, and you would wake up laughing.

Meanwhile, pop star Linda Ronstadt (whose former beau was onetime California governor Jerry Brown) was taking an interest in Jim that was beyond the professional. Even Debbie Pearl, who had introduced them, was surprised by the romance that ensued. Ronstadt, after all, was thirty-seven years old at the time, and Jim was only twenty-one. Ronstadt not only dropped in to the Comedy Store regularly and signed Jim to tour with her, she even went to Calgary to visit him while he was filming *Finders Keepers*. And the relationship became more intense that fall when they were both back in Los Angeles.

The Duck Factory's Jay Tarses recalls Jim as a good-natured, talented kid who was always a pleasure to work with. "This seemed like a good project," says Tarses. "We had fun, and we all thought we were doing good work." According to Tarses, "Jim was a good guy, very warm and genuine, who was very popular with the cast and crew. He had boundless energy, and at every opportunity he would entertain people with his uncanny impressions. In between takes, the rest of us might be sitting around having coffee or reading newspapers. Jim's instinct would be to do something amusing. It got to the point where sometimes you wanted to say, 'Jim, I'm trying to read. Would you please just shut up and let me sit here?'"

Jim was extremely eager to do a good job and make a good impression on his colleagues, and he succeeded. Jack Gilford, who had been in the theater for fifty years and knew every trick, told Allan Burns it was phenomenal that Carrey, doing his first TV series, had such remarkably good instincts as an actor. He was in almost every scene, and, according to Burns, he was impressive not only when he had most of the lines but also in scenes where his job was to react to other actors.

In November, Jim scored another breakthrough on NBC: he finally made his debut on *The Tonight Show*—almost two years after his traumatic non-appearance with Johnny Carson. Now he could be billed as the talented comedian "who can be seen starring in a weekly series on this very network."

Despite his manic behavior on the *Duck Factory* set, Jim was rather shy when it came to discussing his personal life, about which his colleagues knew nothing—until one day he asked fellow cast member Teresa Ganzel if she could give him a ride after work. He wanted to be dropped off at his girlfriend's house. Ganzel was taken aback when Carrey directed her to a mansion in Brentwood, which was secluded behind baronial gates.

"Who lives here?" asked Ganzel.

The answer: Linda Ronstadt.

This news created quite a buzz on the *Duck Factory* set, and word of the romance also became the subject of excited speculation in the Toronto media. Ziggy Lorenc was heartbroken when she heard a report about Jim and Linda on the radio. "It wasn't just that he was dating someone else," explains Lorenc, "but Linda Ronstadt happened to be my favorite singer."

In mid-November, *Toronto Star* celebrity columnist Rita Zekas was astonished to receive a phone call from Percy. "I'm Jim Carrey's dad," he said, "and I want to thank you for setting the record straight on Jim's relationship with Linda Ronstadt."

Zekas had expressed skepticism about a report published in her own newspaper that the two were living in Ronstadt's mansion in unwedded bliss.

"They're just good friends," Percy assured Zekas. "And they're not living together."

Then Percy went on to give Zekas a scoop on another development. Percy and Kay were planning to fly to Los Angeles the next week to move in with Jim.

"It's a heady thing for a kid his age," Percy explained. "Jim has asked us to move down to keep an eye on him."

Indeed, Jim had asked his parents to move in with him. It was a decision he would come to regret.

tHE **p**ARTY'S **O**VER

STILL **TORN** between his wish for independence and his desire to please Percy and Kay, Jim decided he was now in a position to make his parents' dreams come true. They had always wanted to live in Los Angeles, which to them was the center of show-business glamour, but it had always seemed off-limits, even after Jim had moved there. In truth, Jim was sending his parents a mixed message. On the one hand, he loved being on his own and not being subject to their control. On the other hand, he yearned to bask in their approval of what he had achieved. He was earning good money, his future seemed rosy, and he had a bungalow in North Hollywood with a spare bedroom. In a burst of generosity, he decided to share his good fortune with the two people he cared about most.

It would take him a long time to come to terms with what his motivations were. More than a decade later, in 1995, he told Barbara Walters in a widely seen ABC television interview: "I was trying too hard to be the good son. I wanted to be like Elvis. 'I bought you Graceland, Mom.'"

At first all three of them enjoyed the novelty. But while Jim was going to work every day shooting *The Duck Factory*, Percy and Kay didn't know anyone in L.A., and they had nowhere to go. Percy busied himself as much as possible doing Jim's bookkeeping. A few times Jim took his parents to the *Duck Factory* set in Studio City, where they mostly sat quietly and exchanged uneasy chitchat with Jim's colleagues. Allan Burns saw Percy as a dark, taciturn person; he never got a glimpse of Percy's jocular side. And Kay seemed painfully shy.

On most days, Percy and Kay stayed at Jim's house watching television and chainsmoking. It wasn't long before they were getting on Jim's nerves. And to make matters worse, Kay suffered from angina and arthritis, and her health problems became more acute.

In December 1983, Jim began to wonder whether things were starting to unravel. His romance with Linda Ronstadt had come to an end, leaving him in a funk. (She started seeing George Lucas.) While hanging out at Linda's house in Brentwood, Jim had savored his first taste of the perks that come along with stardom—famous friends, limos at the door, constant deference—and he enjoyed it unreservedly. But he was deeply distressed by the media attention, which he kept saying had blown things out of proportion. After all he had done during his first year in L.A., it bothered him to be known as Ronstadt's boyfriend.

At the same time, Jim's involvement with Linda was proving a bit awkward for David Holiff, who had been initially responsible for bringing them together through Debbie Pearl. David hated having to call Jim at Linda's house. And that was not the only source of tension between them. They still had no contract. A few months earlier, when everything seemed to be going spectacularly well, Holiff had asked Jim: "Are you happy with the way things are going?" Jim replied that he was very happy. David seized the opportunity to raise the matter of a contract again, and Jim replied: "Relax, David. When things are good, why complicate them?"

Holiff had kept Jim so busy, working at a frantic pace ever since they'd arrived in L.A., that Jim was starting to feel more than a little exhausted. And David's style of relentless hustling, which had seemed such a positive factor at the beginning of their association, was starting to become an irritation.

Jim was no longer relying exclusively on David for guidance. The more successful he became, the more people he had offering advice on how to shape his career. Among them was Chris Albrecht, then a talent agent at International Creative Management (ICM), who had started working for Jim at David's suggestion. Having once been co-owner of a comedy club, Albrecht was one of the few people who understood both the comedy business and the Hollywood world of film and TV.

Tensions escalated with the arrival of Percy, because Holiff still felt that Jim's father disliked him, and he suspected that the elder Carrey would try to undermine Jim's confidence in him. Holiff's fears were not unfounded. Percy thought Jim needed a big-time manager—and David's reputation wasn't starry enough to match Percy's ambitions for his son. In December, Jim told David that he wanted a change. He had stopped appearing at the Comedy Store. He didn't want to do impressions, he explained, because by doing imitations of other people, he had lost touch with the real Jim Carrey.

A lot of people were baffled by what seemed like an inexplicable change in Jim. "Has he lost his mind?" Mitzi Shore asked David Holiff.

"I just can't continue doing what I've been doing," Jim told David. He had started therapy, and he was taking acting classes. He felt it was time to do some exploring, and it was clear he was going through some personal pain. It was also clear that this was the end of the line for Holiff as Carrey's manager.

There was no fight over money, as there had been when Howie Mandel dropped Holiff. Jim paid David all the commissions he was owed, including a cut of his *Duck Factory* salary. Nonetheless, Holiff was in shock. He couldn't believe, after all he had done to put Jim Carrey in orbit, that Jim was going to walk away.

But according to Debbie Pearl, it wasn't all that surprising. "There aren't a lot of Hollywood partnerships that could survive the kind of transition strain that Jim was going through. He was young, and he was being pulled in a lot of different directions. There were a lot of people around giving him ideas and turning his head. And unfortunately, dealing with David wasn't easy for Jim. Being the kind of person who bangs down doors and forces people to pay attention, which David was, is no longer an asset once the person you're working with has reached a certain point and is having a hard time dealing with the pressure."

Meanwhile, back at *The Duck Factory*, the ebullient mood of those who felt sure they had a winner was giving way to a state of increasing uncertainty and anxiety. After seeing the first couple of episodes, Brandon Tartikoff at NBC was pressing Allan Burns to get the show ready as soon as possible. As the show had originally been conceived, a lot of technically complex cartoon footage would be incorporated with the live-action sequences. Burns told Tartikoff he had to wait for the animation sequences to come in, and the show couldn't be rushed.

"We've got to get it on the air," said Tartikoff. He wanted to put the show into NBC's schedule before the end of November. Burns said that just wouldn't be possible.

Because of technical problems and escalating costs (the budget, at $400,000 per episode, was notably high), Burns eventually had to drop most of the animation bits. But many key decisions had been made for the sake of having them. If it weren't for the cartoon inserts, he might have opted for a live studio audience and more than one camera. And if it weren't for the difficulties of mixing animation with live action, the show could have been delivered to the network much sooner.

By the time the show was delivered, Burns started to pick up signals that something had gone seriously awry. He had been expecting the show to go to air in January, but when the network schedule for January was issued, there was no sign of *The Duck Factory*.

In the interim, Tartikoff had screened a few episodes for his boss, Grant Tinker—and Tinker was not pleased.

Having heard nothing, Burns called Tinker directly and asked: "Grant, what's going on?"

His old friend replied: "What's going on is that I've seen your show and I don't like it. I don't think anyone in it is very good."

This conversation put a huge strain on an old friendship; though Burns and Tinker would eventually have a rapprochement, the rupture lasted for years.

Tartikoff and Jeff Sagansky remained supporters of the show, but, given Tinker's reaction, they all knew it was a losing battle. The network waited until late April to put the show on the air. It ran on NBC's strongest night, Thursday, at 9:30 p.m., sandwiched between *Cheers* and *Hill Street Blues*—but because it was so late in the season those shows were mostly in reruns. *Duck Factory* replaced *Buffalo Bill*, a controversial show that didn't have enough heart to hold the audience delivered by *Cheers*.

The reviews for *Duck Factory* were not terrible, but few of them were glowing, either. The show was charming in a quirky, old-fashioned way, and it dealt with amusingly eccentric characters and recognizable emotions. But it was perhaps too low-key. If Burns had been able to include the cartoon sequences he'd originally envisioned, maybe that would have been enough of a novelty to carry the show.

As Skip Tarkenton, Jim Carrey showed tremendous charm and style. The camera loved him, and despite being a novice among a cast of veterans, Jim more than anyone made the show seem fresh. This was not mugging, this was not stand-up, this was not doing impressions. Jim Carrey was playing a character, and his acting ability was impressive.

Arriving from Duluth just in time to attend the funeral of the *Duck Factory*'s owner, Skip quickly has to come to terms with the fact that Buddy Winkler was a sleazebag who exploited his employees and turned them into a kind of dysfunctional family— a band of likable neurotics. The first episode got the series off to a great start with a delicious satire of a hypocritical Hollywood funeral. (It carries echoes of Evelyn Waugh's *The Loved One,* and of the famous comment on the big turnout for the funeral of that much-loathed mogul Harry Cohn: People came to make sure the son of a bitch was really dead.) Unfortunately, the rest of the series couldn't live up to the opening episode. *The Duck Factory* was not often able to reach this level of comic invention. What started out as something fresh and original deteriorated into just another mildly pleasant sitcom.

As the story develops, Skip not only takes a job at the Duck

Factory but, to save money, rents Buddy's private room on the premises. With the best of intentions he keeps getting himself into trouble. It's the kind of office where there are always people waiting for someone to say the wrong thing. The ditzy Mrs. Winkler befriends Skip and then appoints him producer of *Dippy Duck*— much to his embarrassment. Carrey demonstrates a memorably deft comic touch in a scene where he has to endure the silent stares of colleagues who all assume he's reaching for the top by sleeping with the boss's widow.

But Skip Tarkenton was a bit too obviously a male version of Mary Richards (Mary Tyler Moore), and the conception of the character put Jim into a straitjacket. The setup precluded turning Carrey loose to perform the kind of inspired, crazed comedy he was capable of. If Jim had been allowed to make Skip into an edgier, funnier guy, like Robin Williams in *Mork and Mindy*, the show might have had an easier time winning an audience.

In retrospect, Allan Burns regretted that he didn't really get to know Jim Carrey before the role of Skip Tarkenton had been established: "Had I understood Jim's incredible qualities earlier, I would have reshaped the character rather than forcing him to fit into something that had been conceived before he came along. It's unfortunate, but by the time we cast him, there just wasn't time to reinvent the character. We were behind the eight-ball, and we had to get going in a hurry."

After anticipating this breakthrough for almost a year, it came as a definite letdown for Jim when *The Duck Factory* finally reached the air—and was received with less than wild enthusiasm. And a few weeks later, he experienced another disappointment when *Finders Keepers*, the Richard Lester movie he had made in Calgary the previous fall, opened to negative reviews and feeble business.

The movie is a tale of stolen money, frenzied chases, ruthless double-crosses and a game of hide-and-seek stretching from California to Nebraska. The plot turns on a large wad of cash stashed in a coffin in the baggage car of a train. Several Alberta towns— including Red Deer, Lethbridge and High River—served as stand-ins for outposts of the American West. And the action stunts involved not only Via Rail trains but a house that gets towed from one place to another.

Michael O'Keefe as the protagonist, a likable hustler on the lam, is surrounded by some wonderfully talented and well-known actors—Beverly D'Angelo as a beguilingly flaky stranger on a train, Louis Gossett Jr. as a brilliant conman, Brian Dennehy as a cranky small-town mayor and David Wayne as an elderly train conductor. But the movie was not destined to be one of Lester's hits. *Variety* described *Finders Keepers* as "frantic," "uneven," "maddening" and "artless."

Jim Carrey has just a few minutes of screen time near the end of the film, playing a lunkheaded army deserter whose relatives keep him hidden so he won't be arrested. When a coffin supposedly containing his corpse arrives, it becomes a conspicuous problem that he's still walking around, talking nonsense as usual. The best that could be said of Carrey was that he did a competent job portraying a young moron.

The movie itself more or less arrived in a box. This was not the kind of role that was going to result in a career breakthrough— especially since *Finders Keepers* disappeared from theaters with unseemly haste.

By the time the thirteenth and final episode of *The Duck Factory* was telecast on July 11, it had become clear that the show was not the triumph that Jim Carrey had been hoping for. Ironically, in the final episode of the show, Jim as Skip bears a heavy burden of responsibility because all of his colleagues are counting on him to persuade a TV network to renew their cartoon show *Dippy Duck*. By then, almost no one was counting on the renewal of *The Duck Factory*.

"People had already seen the handwriting on the wall," says Burns. "Typically the networks don't have the courtesy to call and tell you your show isn't being renewed. Instead you get the news from your agent, who calls and says: 'The schedule is out, and your show isn't on it.'"

That was the way it had been when CBS yanked *Lou Grant* after five seasons of Emmy and Peabody awards. And that's the way it was with NBC and *The Duck Factory*. After winning six Emmys and creating several legendary shows, Allan Burns had reached a dead end in his TV career. And Jim Carrey found himself right back where he had been more than a year earlier, when he landed at the Comedy Store.

Jim had lost his career momentum and he was not in a good state of mind to handle it. His heart really wasn't into going back to his old act. Coping with a tremendous amount of psychological baggage that summer, he tried to pull himself together and put the best face on things.

In June, while the show was still on the air, Carrey admitted in an interview with Noel Gallagher of the *London Free Press* that the show was unlikely to be renewed—but refused to be dismayed by its expected demise. "TV is such a shot in the dark," he said. "I know this is a quality show no matter what happens to it. I suppose I'd be upset if I were forty and my series was dying, but it's too early in my career to worry."

By then, he had new management. David Holiff had been

replaced by one of the highest-profile companies in show business: Rollins, Joffe, Morra and Brezner. The original New York arm of the company handled Woody Allen and David Letterman. The newer L.A. branch handled Robin Williams, among others. Carrey was being handled by David Steinberg (no relation to the comedian of that name), and the goal was to get Carrey another series.

Lucy Dervaitis, Jim's grade-seven teacher in Burlington, had written him a letter after seeing *Duck Factory*, and in October she received a reply, written in the style of a conscientious student on both sides of a piece of lined paper. She'd enclosed a copy of the caricature he'd drawn of her, handing out detentions; he was delighted to see it, and described it in his letter back as "the work of a disturbed child—me!" Unfortunately, he reported, *The Duck Factory* had been canceled. But the experience of making it, he insisted, was wonderful. And now Warner Brothers was developing a new pilot for him. (Nothing ever came of it.) Along with the letter, Jim sent an autographed picture for Lucy's children.

In November, Jim and Lucy were reunited when she came to see his show at the Imperial Room of the Royal York Hotel, and he invited her to visit his dressing room after the show for a glass of champagne.

The Toronto gig put some much-needed cash in Jim's pocket, but creatively it was hardly one of the high points of his career. Carrey had a looser, more casual look; instead of a suit and tie, he wore red pants with a black-and-white striped shirt. Hometown critics who had once pulled out all the superlatives to describe Jim were beginning to seem bored by his too-familiar bag of tricks.

"Because he's Jim Carrey, this is enough to get by," Rob Salem remarked in the *Star*, "but not enough to get ahead."

Bob Thompson of the *Toronto Sun* offered a harsher judgment: "His return to Toronto was so disappointing." According to Thompson, there were more misses than hits in Carrey's lineup of impressions, with few innovative adventures and too many pat postures. "Sadly he's on the verge of becoming a self-indulgent parody mugging away his abilities on the cheap theatrics that guarantee easy laughs."

The truth was that Jim Carrey had already decided it was time to stop doing impressions. He knew he was going to have to reinvent himself; he just hadn't yet figured out how.

ELEVEN
o o o o o

bLOODLETTINGS

IN THE FALL of 1984, Jim Carrey co-starred with Rich Little in *Rich Little and Friends*, a one-hour TV variety special set in New Orleans. The show (a Steele-Goulet production directed by Michael Steele for the CBC) opened with the two impressionists from Canada riding through the French Quarter in a red horsedrawn carriage. What triggered the TV special was a stage show conceived as Canada's contribution to the 1984 World's Fair in New Orleans. Parts of that show were filmed and edited into the TV production, which included other sequences in which the stars left the stage and burst onto the streets, especially Bourbon Street.

Operating in peak form, Carrey did a memorable Marlon Brando impression in a takeoff on that greatest of all New Orleans dramas, *A Streetcar Named Desire*. And when Carrey sang, he showed the confidence of a true musical comedy star. While Rich Little impersonated Dean Martin, Jim was marvelous as Jerry Lewis. When Little imitated Bing Crosby singing *Now You Has Jazz* (a Cole

Porter song from the movie *High Society*), Carrey topped him by mimicking all the jazz instruments in the band, one at a time.

Jim was happy to have the $15,000 fee he collected for spending a week in New Orleans, and he certainly conveyed the impression of a guy enjoying himself to the hilt. This was a winning, high-spirited performance. Yet there was a subtext that people watching this show wouldn't have guessed. To Jim, Rich Little's career as the most famous impressionist ever to come out of Canada had become a cautionary tale. He could see where that path would lead—straight to Las Vegas. And nothing was more horrifying to Jim than the prospect of winding up as the next Rich Little.

Jim was starting to understand the side of the Vegas sensibility that Mark Breslin, Mike MacDonald, Sam Kinison and others derided. Vegas was the capital of artificial high spirits, familiar faces doing their tired and predictable old acts night after night. What worked in Vegas was material recycled from vaudeville and old television shows. Vegas was a magnet for tired, pampered rich people with more money than taste. Jim knew that the price of succeeding here was to give up your aspirations to be fresh, daring and original, and pander to the audience. He knew he had cornered himself when he would write a good comedy routine for himself, only to realize it had no place in his impressionist act.

Las Vegas had come to symbolize the career path from which he was trying to escape. One night in Vegas, watching Rich Little's act, Jim had a kind of epiphany. Cary Grant was in the audience that night. Little moved into the audience and stopped at Grant's table, where he lingered and performed his impression of Grant. The star and his guest looked up at Little and applauded rather awkwardly. And at that moment, Jim explained a few years later,

"I realized I didn't want to be the guy doing the Cary Grant impression; I wanted to be Cary Grant."

If *The Duck Factory* had been a hit, Jim would have been able to put his old act behind him gracefully. He was still hoping to make a breakthrough in movies and TV, but while he was marking time there was strong pressure to go back to the impressions, which were a guaranteed audience-pleaser. He knew that if he could dredge up the old enthusiasm he could get standing ovations night after night. But his heart just wasn't in it any longer—and audiences could sense the difference.

Jim's hopes for a new TV series with Warner Brothers came to nothing, but his new managers, Buddy Morra and David Steinberg, landed him his first co-starring role in a movie. The film was a vampire spoof called *Once Bitten*, which was being produced for the Samuel Goldwyn Company with Samuel Goldwyn Jr. as executive producer. The director, Howard Storm, was a former stand-up comic from New York who had been directing TV comedy such as *Mork and Mindy* and *Rhoda*. Lauren Hutton, the husky-voiced former model, had been cast as a vampire—a voracious countess who can survive only if she drinks the blood of a virginal teenage boy.

Carrey had been recommended by Storm's friend Allan Burns, creator of *The Duck Factory*, who had hired Storm in the 1970s to direct six episodes of *Rhoda*. And Storm also had a connection with Carrey through Rollins, Joffe, Morra and Brezner. Storm knew Buddy Morra very well, and also had a long association with company founder Jack Rollins, who had guided him through his career as a comedy performer (including a stint in San Francisco with the satiric group The Committee). Rollins was best known as the man who handled Woody Allen, and Storm had worked on several Allen movies, both as assistant director and as an actor. Just before directing *Once Bitten*, Storm had appeared in *Broadway Danny Rose* as one of the veteran comedians telling the story of Danny Rose while sitting around a table at the Carnegie Deli in New York.

"We were searching for a young actor who could handle comedy but who would also be credible in the role of a teenage boy just graduating from high school," Storm recalls. "It wasn't an easy role to cast, and we had looked at a lot of people—the standard list of young comedy actors—before we settled on Jim. He was good-looking, he could act, and he was a pleasure to deal with. I hadn't seen his stage act, but I could tell he had a gift for physical comedy, like Jerry Lewis, and was a throwback to vaudeville. Jim seemed refreshingly different from other young comics of the day—who had a tendency to be hipper-than-thou. Jim was not only talented, he was very professional in his behavior. We were very impressed."

Once Bitten was being made on a tight schedule (nine weeks) and a tight budget ($2.5 million). Eventually that was stretched to eleven weeks and $3.2 million. During the shoot, Storm encountered a couple of difficulties. One was a conflict with Lauren Hutton, who sometimes tried to change her appearance from one shot to the next. Another concerned Cleavon Little, who played her faithful valet. Little—a stage actor who had became a Hollywood name when Mel Brooks chose him as the lead in *Blazing Saddles*—had the funniest role as a kind of gay black version of the Erich von Stroheim character in *Sunset Boulevard*. But during filming, Little became seriously ill, and Storm had to rearrange scenes accordingly.

The biggest problem facing Storm was the anemic script. The material was meant to be a hip, funny new spin on *Dracula,* combining the horror-spoof genre with a teenage romantic comedy.

Rita and Jim on a school trip to Ontario Legislature (courtesy of Lucy Belvedere)

1984 reunion with former teacher Lucy Dervaitis (Belvedere)
(courtesy of Lucy Belvedere)

Former managers Leatrice Spevack and Demi Thompson
(courtesy of Leatrice Spevack)

As King Tut in 1982 Ontario lottery TV commercial
(courtesy of Alan Marr)

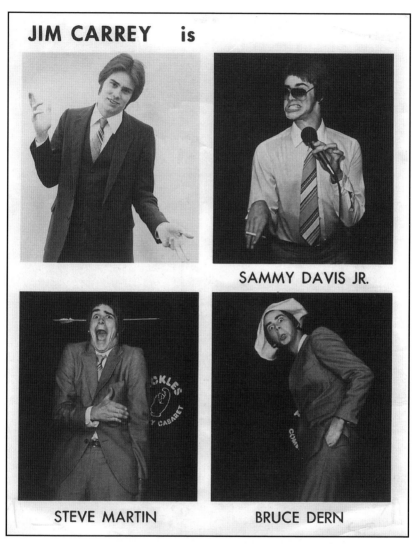

Promotion for Carrey's impressionist act
(courtesy of Leatrice Spevack and Just for Laughs)

Film debut in *Introducing Janet* (1981)
(courtesy of CBC and Glen Salzman)

Performing in Toronto, 1989 (photo by Louis De Filippis)

Earth Girls Are Easy

Ace Ventura: When Nature Calls

Ace Ventura: Pet Detective

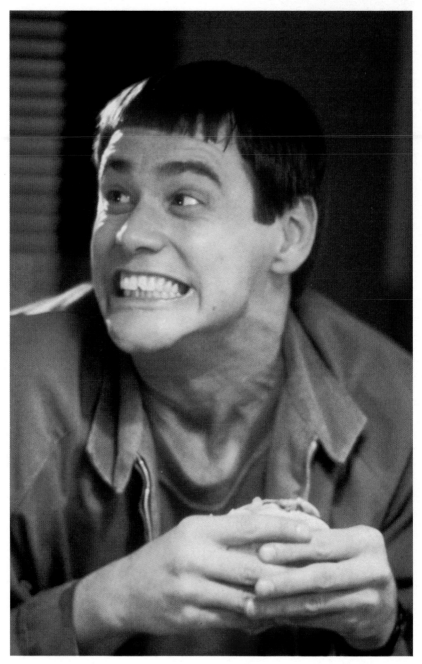

Dumb and Dumber

Batman Forever

The Cable Guy

The Truman Show

The Truman Show

With Lauren Holly (photo by Thomas Lawlor/Shooting Star)

With daughter Jane and Lauren Holly at Mann's Chinese Theatre, 1995
(photo by Ron Davis/Shooting Star)

The storyline was more than slightly reminiscent of the 1979 George Hamilton comedy *Love at First Bite*, with the genders reversed. As the world's most glamorous vampire, Hutton presides in decadent hilltop Art Deco luxury looking down on all Los Angeles, pampered by various attendants who have been serving her for centuries. But she is finding it increasingly difficult to find fresh male virgins, whose blood is essential to preserving her eternal youth. And she must partake three times before Hallowe'en or start looking her age (four hundred years).

By day the countess sleeps in a coffin, clad in a trendy workout outfit. By night she cruises L.A.'s hottest nightspots. That's where she meets Mark Kendall (Carrey's character), who has come to Hollywood, accompanied by a couple of pals from the suburbs, looking for action because his girlfriend Robin (Karen Kopins) is not ready to "go all the way."

Unlike traditional vampires, who were in the habit of biting necks, the countess has to bite Mark on the inner thigh—and she has to do it three times. After his first tryst with her, Mark returns home in a state of considerable confusion, not quite sure what has happened to him. But parents and schoolfriends are alarmed to notice certain unsettling new habits, such as Mark's sudden appetite for raw meat.

Storm and the actors had high hopes for the movie, but it's not a whole lot of fun to watch, except for the decor, bits of Little's performance and an outstanding masquerade dance sequence. Carrey is good-natured and likable, but he's stuck in a naive straight-man part; he's required to be as bland and pretty as Tab Hunter or Russ Tamblyn. Apart from a sequence lasting mere seconds in which he slips in a parody of Robert DeNiro, Carrey is given little chance to unleash his wild-and-crazy side. His character is not allowed to have much of a personality beyond awkward, mixed-up, sex-starved boy next door.

Once Bitten got mostly negative reviews when it was released in November. "It has more stylishness than wit," wrote Janet Maslin in the *New York Times*. "The film affects a glossy sophisticated look that does little to upgrade its adolescent humor."

Nevertheless, the movie played in theaters all over North America for four or five weeks and did moderately well at the box office, grossing $6.5 million in its first week. It fared even better on video and made money for Goldwyn. But hardly anyone remembers it fondly. Such was its legacy that Howard Storm has not directed another movie. And it did absolutely nothing for Jim Carrey's career, leaving him in limbo. It's hard to imagine an actor as hungry as Jim was saying no to a leading role in a Hollywood movie, but he learned a lesson that he filed away for later use, when he had more options: exposure alone is of little value if it doesn't provide an opportunity to show off what you do best.

By the time *Once Bitten* was released, Jim had already finished shooting another movie—*Peggy Sue Got Married*, directed by Francis Coppola (who had been a Hollywood legend ever since making the first two *Godfather* movies a decade earlier, but had stumbled badly more recently). Written by husband-and-wife team Jerry Leichtling and Arlene Sarner, the movie is a time-travel romantic comedy about a forty-three-year-old woman who, after passing out at her twenty-fifth anniversary class reunion, goes back to her senior year in high school circa 1960 and reconnects with a world about to be shaken by the arrival of the Beatles, the failure of the Edsel and the birth of feminism. The project had the kind of troubled history that usually proves fatal. Before Coppola agreed to direct it with Kathleen Turner in the title role, the original star,

Debra Winger, and two well-known directors, Peggy Marshall and Jonathan Demme, had defected. And it was beaten to the screen by another time-travel comedy, *Back to the Future*.

Kathleen Turner plays Peggy Sue with a breathy, world-weary manner, and somehow manages to carry the picture without ever being convincing as an eighteen-year-old. Of course it helps that her bewildered parents are wonderfully portrayed by Barbara Harris and Don Murray. But the big question facing Peggy Sue is whether she should marry her hotshot boyfriend Charlie, knowing that he won't really have the singing career he dreams of but will wind up running his father's appliance business and doing embarrassingly tacky commercials on TV.

As Charlie, Nicolas Cage—with blond hair, a false nose and false teeth—catches the desperate eagerness of the character, but he doesn't seem to be on the same planet as Turner's Peggy Sue, and it's hard to imagine them as a couple. Cage was a nephew of the director (he had recently changed his name from Nicolas Coppola), and at this stage of his career he was relatively unknown. But it was clear he had talent and drive, that he was an actor who was going places.

Jim was very excited about being involved in a movie that had such a famous and distinguished director. *Peggy Sue* was the fifth movie he had made, and the most notable so far, yet it too failed to advance his career. Playing one of Charlie's high school pals, a future cocaine-snorting dentist named Walter Getz who wears wire-rimmed glasses, Carrey simply didn't have enough time on the screen to earn much attention from the audience. There's a flash of Carrey's goofiness when Walter and Charlie perform a doo-wop rendition of the song *I Wonder Why* as part of a male quintet; Carrey looks terrific in a silver jacket and seems ready to roll, but the scene goes by too quickly. When the movie was belatedly released in the fall of 1986, it attracted a lot of favorable attention—but Carrey's appearance was hardly noticed. He was overshadowed not only by Cage but also by Barry Miller as the brooding nerd of the class.

As usual, Carrey took on the task of entertaining the cast and crew, which made him very popular on the set. It is not unusual for actors thrown together on a film set to become friends, but often these friendships don't last beyond the shooting schedule. The rapport Cage and Carrey established was deeper than that. In Cage (two years his junior), Carrey saw someone he could learn from, someone he could talk to and someone he could trust. Playing characters who were buddies, these two hungry young actors became pals in real life. In fact the greatest benefit Carrey derived from appearing in the movie was an enduring friendship with Cage.

And during this period, Carrey felt a need for friends he could count on. He seemed to be doing a little time-traveling of his own. Going through a difficult time in his life, he found that current setbacks reverberated with reminders of the trauma he had suffered as a teenager almost a decade earlier, when Percy lost his job and the whole family wound up as slaves in a nightmarish factory. If he was overreacting to the problems he was facing now, it was perhaps because he was having a delayed reaction to what had happened much earlier.

Consequently, Jim's relationship with his parents reached the breaking point. He was running out of money, and his patience was wearing thin. Things got so bad that Jim dreaded going home, because Percy and Kay would be there, smoking and talking and watching whatever happened to be on TV. During this period, as Jim confided ten years later to *Rolling Stone* writer Fred Schruers, he had dreams in which he was strangling his mother. Besides, Kay's health was deteriorating (she feared an attack of pleurisy), and the cost of getting her medical treatment in the United States was formidable. Given the uncertainty of his career, Jim no longer felt he was in a position to support his parents. And he didn't feel emotionally capable of having them around.

Finally he made a painful decision. He told Percy and Kay he needed to be on his own, he could not handle the burden of supporting them, and after living with Jim for more than a year, it was time for them to go home. It was a traumatic parting for all three of them. As Jim later explained, he had to come to terms with the fact that he was really angry at his parents for everything that had happened and for the burden he had taken on.

This was an excruciating period for Jim. He was going broke, and he realized that, in the eyes of some people, he was washed up at the age of twenty-three. He had little idea where he was heading, and that scared him. Jim's success wasn't just for himself. It had been a way of pleasing Percy and Kay, of giving them some payback for the years of misery the whole family had endured. For five years he had been on a roll, moving ever upward toward his dream. Now with the failure of *The Duck Factory*, compounded by the failure of *Once Bitten* and his loss of faith in the act that had once earned standing ovations, Jim had to face some devastating questions: Were the good times over? Was the great future he had been striving toward for so long already in fact behind him? Was it possible he wasn't going to become a great star after all? Percy and Kay went back to Canada, somewhat bewildered and saddened. They were still fervent believers in Jim's career, but their chatter about it had become an irritation, because, for the first time, Jim himself was losing faith in the dream that stardom was his destiny.

Although he would still play the manic clown with people he didn't know very well, Jim was becoming quieter and more withdrawn with people he knew better. He was going through the motions. He would go to a lot of movies, he would take acting classes, he would work out at the gym, he would date occasionally. He had started making eccentric sculptures as a kind of art therapy. Some nights he would hang out at the Comedy Store, although his appearances onstage became infrequent. And on Sundays he would play baseball with some musician friends.

According to Buddy Morra, his manager at the time, Jim was suffering from a severe loss of confidence in himself. This was partly because he was giving up his impressions, which had always brought him laughter and applause. And while he wasn't prepared to go on doing the act that earned him such a warm response, it was hard for him to live without the feedback that used to come with it.

Morra wonders whether he and his colleagues gave Carrey the wrong advice when they encouraged him to drop his impressions and develop a new act. "The old act gave Jim a leg up when people came to see him," Morra recalls. "They might be setting up an audition, and if they'd seen Jim onstage they had a favorable impression that carried over to the audition. When at our request he stopped doing the old act, he lost that advantage. For a while, nothing seemed to be working. It's much easier to get a first shot at success, which he'd already had. But he was finding that getting that second shot can be really tough."

bETWEEN **p**ROJECTS

WITHIN THE small circle of comedians who hung
out together at the Comedy Store and often stayed up most of the
night after the club closed, none had a greater influence on Jim
Carrey than the dark and daring Sam Kinison. A former
Pentecostal preacher, Kinison had begun his career touring
churches all over the United States with his brothers—only to discover that his real pulpit was in the comedy clubs that had begun
springing up by the late 1970s. Kinison had already become a fix-
ture on the L.A. comedy scene by the time Carrey arrived in 1983.
His rants about sex, religion and politics had made him a legend
among comedy-world insiders, even though he was considered so
far from the mainstream that Mitzi Shore would always schedule
Sam to appear last, after midnight, when the kind of customers
who would be horrified had already gone home, leaving only a
smattering of hard-core adventurers seeking something wild.

Sam's fans adored his trademark style of delivery. A rather
bulky, rumpled-looking fellow, he would begin talking slowly and

quietly, wearing an oversize overcoat and a beret, possibly dropping a few quotes from the Bible while warming up. All the while
he would pace the stage menacingly, like a caged lion making a final
attempt to control his temper. Then his raspy voice would build to
a screaming crescendo, as his rage finally exploded. As often as not,
the target would be women who were doing him wrong or driving
him crazy. His best-known rant was known as "the bitch from hell."
Some people found Kinison frightening and deeply unpleasant, but
there was also a streak of genuine brilliance. Beyond the politically
incorrect cracks and the torrents of abuse, his fans glimpsed something more: a breathtaking honesty about his own failings,
appetites and hypocrisies; a refusal to charm the audience; and a
readiness to send up his own anger as a kind of campy excess.

Eight years older than Carrey, Kinison became a kind of
mentor to the kid from Canada, even though Carrey's sweet showbiz impressions were light years from Kinison's corrosive social
satire. That was something Sam would kid Jim about. Unlike
Andrew Dice Clay—who became prominent around the same
time, and truly was vicious—Sam could be completely charming.
He had charisma, and he could win people over. In the early years
of their friendship, Carrey worshipped Kinison without making
any moves to be a follower of the gospel according to Sam, either
in his personal life or in his act. Offstage, Sam could be thoughtful
and charitable, but he was also reckless and self-destructive. Hard
drinking, drugs and partying-till-you-drop were all part of his
scene.

It was when Jim returned to the Comedy Store after *Duck
Factory*, *Once Bitten* and *Peggy Sue Got Married* that the influence of
Sam Kinison began to show up in his performances. Among those
who had a close-up view of that transition was Kelly Moran,

a former telephone company technician from Texas. Moran was already dabbling in comedy and would later become a full-time comedian, but his job at the Comedy Store from mid-1985 to late 1987 did not involve being funny. Four nights a week he played the piano—while getting an education by watching an array of comics perform.

While making music at the Comedy Store, Moran picked up a realistic overview of the comedy world. There was a lot of talk about the legendary stars who had once been unknowns working the room—Robin Williams, Richard Pryor and Eddie Murphy, among others. But L.A. was a town of ten-minute appearances, and for every star of the future discovered by Mitzi there were scores destined for careers of relative obscurity—comics who would never get that big break in film or TV, never cross over to that next level of success. Instead they would go on, year after year, spending half their time on the road playing towns less glamorous than L.A. and New York, getting paid badly while becoming less hopeful as the years went by, and less capable of connecting with increasingly young audiences. Some of them would give up and drift away from the comedy business altogether; some would destroy themselves with drugs and booze; and a few lucky ones would segue into lucrative gigs on the corporate circuit, or a long-term development deal writing for film or TV that would allow them a measure of comfort and security that still fell short of fame or stardom.

When Moran first knew Jim Carrey, he would often see him at the club in the company of Melissa Womer, an aspiring actress from Pennsylvania who had taken a job as a waitress there. This wasn't her only job; she also worked as a masseuse at a health club. In the comedy world, it's standard practice for comedians to date waitresses working at the club, so no one was surprised about Jim and Melissa—although people were aware that Jim's ex-girlfriend was a famous rock star, while his new girlfriend was somewhat less glamorous. Kelly once made the mistake of asking Jim about Linda Ronstadt, because he was married to a singer who was a big Ronstadt fan. Jim was very guarded and made it clear that he didn't want to talk about her.

"I'd heard a lot about Jim," Moran says. "Then after I met him I was a witness to a turning point in his career, when he was abandoning his impressionist act. He was going through a very dark period."

In fact, Carrey was having a nervous breakdown. Having sent Percy and Kay back to Canada, Jim was still trying to come to terms with the conflicting feelings he had about his parents. He had never stopped trying to please them, and often talked about them with affection. But he also saw them as the cause of a deep malaise within himself that no amount of manic comedy could expunge. This conflict found expression in disturbing paintings with a touch of Dali-like surrealism. Jim's paintings depicted everything from stuffed animals to Percy looking at his watch while holding a gun in his hand.

When Jim's sister Rita came to Los Angeles. for a visit, she took a look at the paintings and asked Jim: "Are you okay?"

To which he retorted: "Yeah, I'm okay. I have an outlet. What do you do?"

Years later, Carrey explained how he was influenced by Kinison's no-holds-barred style. "Sam made me sit back and say, 'Here's a guy who is really doing something different and challenging the audience.' Night after night I saw him chase people out of the Comedy Store. And I thought, if you're willing to take a risk like that, then you're going to do something different with your art."

Inspired by Sam, Jim decided to try playing without a net. At this point, he had no money, he had no job, and he had no act. But he had become aware of the stigma of being an impressionist. You were considered a kind of parasite, living vicariously on the personalities of the celebrities you portrayed. Carrey wanted to be an original the way Sam was an original. The difference between his old act and his new act was the anger he was now expressing. As he later observed, "When I went back to stand-up it was with what nobody wanted me to do, which was ideas."

According to Moran, the transition didn't happen all at once. "Jim would bomb 70 percent of the time. He would get up with no script and free-associate; he would call it 'being in the moment.' And most nights the audience wasn't buying it. On a slow night, he wouldn't care if the audience wasn't going along with him. But on some nights, I would see him revert to his impressionist act, just to avoid a complete disaster. Let's say it's a Friday night and there are a couple of hundred people in the room. You don't want to empty the room; it's not a good thing to do. And if he could see his material wasn't going over, then just to hold the crowd and save his ego, he would slip in his impressions."

But Moran also observed some amazing performances that the public didn't get a chance to see. Before the show went on, Carrey would do things onstage for just a few colleagues—Kelly, the waitresses, other comedians. First would come Carrey's warning: "You're about to see the scariest thing you've ever seen in showbiz." Then Kelly would be asked to play something eerie on the piano. And suddenly Jim would pop up in a chair smoking a cigarette, smiling broadly, and proclaim: "I'm in between projects now."

That was his satiric take on where he was at the moment. "And he was sharing it with a few people who would understand it," Moran recalls. "I would see a free-spirited, completely brilliant show. Jim's commitment to what he was doing was so intense it wouldn't matter to him if there were only three people in the room."

According to Moran, Jim looked for a while like someone who was not taking care of himself, and his wardrobe seemed to consist of not much more than six T-shirts. But everyone knew Jim was going through a bad period, and he got a lot of support from people at the Comedy Store, including Mitzi. Some thought it was Jim's neediness that drew him to Melissa—whose Cybill-Shepherd all-American-girl looks were offset by a very strong, take-control kind of personality.

"As soon as I saw him, he seemed like family," Melissa told a magazine writer. When she first encountered him at the Comedy Store, she was struck by the brilliance of even his offhand repartee with the other comics. Later she watched him sink into a depression. As she explained to Fred Schruers of *Rolling Stone* a decade later, Jim was sometimes so dejected that he would sit on the floor and howl. "I would sit up counselling him until four or five in the morning on many, many nights," she recalled. "At night he has to face himself, and he so does not want to, that the adrenaline rushes up in him."

It was the adrenaline that got him back onto the stage. And it was wrestling with demons that drew him to Sam's dark, visionary comedy. Kinison still had his entourage of what Moran calls "bad-boy, rock-n-roll comics" who were very much in evidence at the late-night revels. People might hang around the Comedy Store after closing, until 2:00 or 2.30 a.m., then move to a spot named Ben Frank's or to Mitzi's house. Certain women—dancers and strippers—would join the group night after night. A woman who had been on the arm of one comedian on Tuesday might turn up on the arm of another comedian on Wednesday.

What made this an unpleasant time in Kelly's recollection was the overriding tension created by cocaine. "I didn't like drugs, but most people at the time were doing coke," he explains. "Jim wasn't, and that made him unusual. I think Jim had too many issues going on inside him to work them out with booze or drugs. Jim and Sam enjoyed each other's company—they genuinely made each other laugh—but Jim didn't follow Sam into a dangerous drug place. Probably the biggest influence that Sam had on Jim was in feeling free to talk about taboo subjects like incest and necrophilia."

Unlike Sam and Jim, Kelly felt his own upbringing was too conventional to provide the kind of material that works in a comedy club. "My childhood was too normal. I'm not fucked up enough," he says, only half jokingly. From the viewpoint of other comedians, one of the qualities that made Jim enviable was that he had such huge personal issues to work with.

"Jim was not very educated, not what you would call book-smart," says Moran, "but he was quite insightful. At first he seemed sort of embarrassed about having worked at Titan Wheels and lived in a camper van. But he learned to talk about it onstage, and that was a big breakthrough. He was eager to learn and grow creatively. There was a part of him that was still a frightened child, because of his background. It was through doing his free-associating act that he was able to confront his fears. He had an intense kind of concentration. His commitment to a character was truly awesome. And I think the reason was that capturing those characters so intensely was his way of escaping reality. It was his way of finding a release from his demons."

In fact, the intensity could be expressed in a startling way onstage. Jim Carrey was the only comedian that Kelly Moran has ever known to shed tears onstage. It didn't happen all the time, but Kelly saw Jim cry about a dozen times.

Perhaps Sam Kinison's influence on Jim could be most clearly observed in a routine Jim sometimes did about the horrors of contemporary dating. He developed a routine about a man whose penis was leading him astray. Jim had a kind of posture that illustrated the point. He would manage a contortion which allowed him to move across the stage while his back appeared to be horizontal, parallel to the floor—like a man who was reluctantly being dragged along by a runaway penis. Then he would say something like: "Hi! My penis and I would like to meet you."

Some nights Carrey would stare defiantly at the crowd and ramble on aimlessly while the audience stared back, silent and perplexed. Sometimes Carrey would do bizarre stunts to demonstrate what it felt like to be dying onstage. More than once he acted the part of a cockroach, crawling across the stage and looking for a crevice where he could take shelter. Sometimes when he bombed he would simply sit on the floor and remark, as if in private conversation with Melissa, "Yeah, honey, pretty soon we're going to be on Easy Street." Then he would start crying.

Carrey's most dramatic feat of creative self-effacement occurred the night he decided to take refuge inside the grand piano that Kelly was playing. The room was about three-quarters full that night, and Jim was delivering one of his rambling, being-in-the-moment monologues.

"He was bombing," Moran recalls. "He was talking in non sequiturs. He was being so far out there that the audience couldn't follow him. There were really only a few chuckles."

That's when Jim decided to express his mortification with a bizarre metaphor. Instead of simply cutting his routine short and leaving the stage, he took refuge inside the piano.

"The piano had a cast-iron frame," Moran explains. "Jim was inside, lying on top of the frame, with his heels on one part of it and his butt on another."

It wasn't easy for Kelly to continue, because Jim's body was muffling the strings of the piano. The comedian who followed Jim, Dom Roland, found it hard to win the attention of the audience; people were more interested in what Jim was doing in the piano. He implored Jim to come out.

"Leave me alone," Jim replied. "I'm just lying in the piano."

"How long are you going to stay in there?" Kelly whispered.

"A while longer," Jim replied.

Each comedian appeared for about ten minutes, and Jim stayed inside the piano through two entire acts, emerging after almost half an hour. He climbed out and walked off the stage slowly.

On March 28, 1987, Jim Carrey ceased to be one of the Comedy Store's most eligible bachelors. He and Melissa were married in Santa Monica. It was an outdoor, New Age ceremony, and Melissa recalled it as an almost perfect day. At sunset the couple wound up crying with happiness.

The following September their daughter Jane was born. Money was tight, and Melissa continued holding two jobs into the eighth month of the pregnancy. Jim was overcome with paternal pride and became a very active and involved father. For a while he led a very domestic life. Despite his Catholic background, he would accompany Melissa to their local Presbyterian church, and even had lunch with the minister.

It might have seemed that Jim had moved into a cozy,

settled-down lifestyle, but he was still dreaming of bigger things. He had a ritual of driving up the long and winding road to the top of Mulholland Drive, where he could look down on all of Los Angeles. The journey represented his ascent to the peaks of Hollywood stardom.

Remembering the conversations about goal-setting he'd had years ago with Ron Scribner at the Café on the Park in Toronto, Jim wrote a check to himself, dated several years in the future. The amount payable to Jim Carrey "for services rendered" was $10 million. It was a bet he was having with himself about the future. He hung onto the check for several years, determined that one day he would be able to cash it.

THIRTEEN

o o o o o

THE COMEBACK KID

AFTER YEARS of featuring Clint Eastwood in his lineup of celebrity impressions, Jim Carrey found in Eastwood an improbable benefactor. Eastwood was hardly known as a promoter of cutting-edge comedy talent, but he took a shine to Carrey after someone slipped him an audition tape in which Jim did his entertaining impression of Clint. As a result, Eastwood, as producer and star, chose Carrey for a small but juicy part in *The Dead Pool*, the fifth and final instalment of his Dirty Harry series. Carrey (billed as James Carrey) grabbed this opportunity with the avidity of Norma Desmond landing her comeback vehicle in *Sunset Boulevard*. No wonder. For the first time, Carrey would be able to display his true talents on the big screen. And even if he hadn't been away from the silver screen for as long as Norma, and he was only twenty-six years old, this was still a comeback of sorts, because Carrey had not been seen by anyone except comedy club audiences for two years.

For once he wasn't cast as a nice, normal boy next door. This was a welcome change, because playing a series of sweet, bland and innocent lads had come close to killing Jim's movie career before it really got started. The role of Johnny Shakes—drug-taking rock singer and first victim in a string of homicides—could have been conceived with Carrey in mind. And once he was cast, Carrey was given liberty by Eastwood and director Buddy Van Horn to embellish the character with his own brilliantly demented touches.

Carrey went about creating this character in much the same way he had developed the routines in his now discarded lineup of singing impressions—with layers and layers of eccentric detail. Johnny Shakes is an unforgettable cartoon of the rock vocalist as rough trade—a charter member of hard-rock café society. A wasted heroin addict, he's outfitted with the accoutrements of hip depravity: tight leather pants, stud bracelets, forked haircut.

We're introduced to Johnny while he's trying to pull himself together for a rock-video film called *Hotel Satan*. It is being put together by a nasty-looking director of slasher films by the name of Peter Swan, portrayed with convincing creepiness by Liam Neeson. It seems that certain deranged game-players are placing bets on the question of which well-known people will be killed. Besides Johnny, the victims include a talk-show host and a middle-aged female film critic who has given Swan a bad review. (Could Eastwood possibly have been inspired by revenge fantasies arising from certain scornful comments from *New Yorker* critic Pauline Kael?) Even Harry himself—San Francisco's celebrity cop/hero— is on the hit list. His survival, as well as the safety of the city, depends on identifying and thwarting the evil genius behind the bizarre murder machine. Swan soon becomes the leading suspect. (In an outlandish case of the pot calling the kettle black,

Harry/Clint blames media sensationalism for the outbreak of violence.) But it turns out the real killer is that lowest of all movie-world creatures, a vindictive screenwriter seeking revenge after having a script rejected.

Bare-chested, with a crucifix hanging around his neck, Carrey as Johnny performs his big number, lip-syncing to the rock band Guns 'N' Roses performing *Welcome to the Jungle*. At the time, the group (which often performed on Sunset Boulevard near the Comedy Store) was relatively obscure. It was Carrey, known in his own circle for his avant-garde taste in rock music, who chose the song—and the movie did much to advance the band's career.

After he retires to his trailer, Johnny gives himself an injection of heroin, which of course is cited by the police and the media as the cause of death. But the audience is witness to the real cause of death, as the ruthless killer pays Johnny a visit and forces poison down his throat. That's Carrey's cue to improvise Johnny's final number—a flamboyant death scene of operatic intensity. By that point, Carrey has had only a few minutes of screen time, and he disappears from the proceedings early on. Yet this is the kind of performance that people remember.

The picture may have been fairly routine action stuff, but it did offer the novelty of a high-speed chase on the famously steep streets of San Francisco, featuring a remote-controlled toy car wired with explosives. And given Clint's track record at the box office, this was a big summer movie (released in July 1988) that was going to be seen by more people than any other film Carrey had been in.

During the shoot, Clint and Jim formed a bond, and a year later, Clint found a way to work Jim into his next movie, *The Pink Cadillac* (also directed by Van Horn). The picture was lackluster even by the standards of Eastwood action movies, and Jim's appearance was so brief that if you went for popcorn you'd miss it. This was less a part than a profile-raising cameo appearance. Still, it did offer a teasing glimpse of Carrey's weird brilliance. At a sleazy bar where Clint tries to pry some information out of Bernadette Peters, the entertainment consists of an Elvis impersonator. And sure enough, there's Jim reprising one of the oldest routines in his inventory of singing impressions—one of the few that he'd found could be successfully reincarnated for the dark, hip new act he was then doing at the Comedy Store. This is not just any old Elvis impersonator; this one is doing Presley as a Thalidomide victim. Singing *Blue Suede Shoes*, Carrey pulls the sleeves of his T-shirt down to make it look as though he has stumps instead of arms, waving them like flippers in time to the music. It's enough to provoke the Bernadette Peters character to walk out, explaining to Clint: "I've had enough of this Elvis tribute."

A few years later, when Carrey became a star, Eastwood was proud of having played a role in promoting his career. Both men kept their mutual admiration society going for years. In 1995, when Carrey was chosen to put his footprints and handprints on the sidewalk in front of Mann's Chinese Theater, Clint was at his side. And in 1996, when Eastwood was given a lifetime achievement award by the American Film Institute, Carrey was emcee for the televised event.

But it was another movie, released the same summer as *The Pink Cadillac,* that showcased Carrey's comedic talents in a leading role for the first time. Hailed by David Denby in *New York* magazine as the most enjoyable bad movie of the year, *Earth Girls Are Easy* was certainly one of the flakiest movies of the 1980s—a goofy, cheerfully scatterbrained, new-wave science-fiction rock musical. Designed in playful and slightly hallucinogenic pastel colors, the movie fitfully tells the story of three furry aliens from the planet Jhazzala. Looking like a trio of wind-up space toys, the aliens—played by Jeff Goldblum, Damon Wayans and Carrey— have an advanced case of cabin fever by the time their spaceship lands in a swimming pool in the San Fernando Valley. Luckily, the swimming pool belongs to Valerie, a delightfully empty-headed manicurist played by that wide-mouthed, long-legged cartoon of screen glamour, Geena Davis, in a role that helped make her a star.

Playing the part of Wiploc, aka Alien #2, Carrey appears initially in a red fur bodysuit with a football helmet and black stripes across his head. He's a wide-eyed adventurer trying to make sense of the local culture and customs while talking what sounds like gibberish (subtitles required) to his two companions. These three guys are not outlandish Spielberg figures; underneath their colorful and hairy exteriors, they're just three horny dudes who are more than ready to party.

As Candy, the owner of the beauty shop where Valerie works, Julie Brown (an MTV personality and co-writer of the script) sings *'Cause I'm a Blonde* and wields her shears like a magic wand. She gives the three aliens a makeover—thus freeing them to pass as furless Valley boys. Joyfully shorn, they get caught up in the fast lanes of L.A. nightlife and the sun-and-surf scene at the beach. There's only one problem; they don't understand the language or what's going on, so they have to make their way by experimenting and imitating.

Of course, when it comes to the comedy of imitation, Jim Carrey is in a class by himself. And when Valerie teaches Wiploc how a toilet works, Carrey's rubber face provides the punchline.

Jim even gets a chance to work his parody of James Dean into the proceedings. After catching *Rebel Without a Cause* on TV, Wiploc adoringly and absurdly mimics Dean's delivery of that unforgettable line: "You're tearing me apart!"

Since Carrey doesn't get to deliver many lines in English, he has limited opportunity in this role to display his amazing vocal dexterity. But that limitation gives him an excuse to operate in the style of a comic from the silent era, making the most of his gift for physical contortions and facial elasticity.

In retrospect, it's amazing, considering the death toll of risky projects in Hollywood, that *Earth Girls* survived the obstacle course. The project had begun with a chat between Julie Brown and British producer Tony Garnett, whose interests were usually in social and political realism. Brown was a songwriter as well as an actress and scriptwriter, and Garnett had the notion that her song *Earth Girls Are Easy* could be the basis of a movie. Fifteen script drafts later, he thought he had a commitment from Warner Brothers. However, Garnett had chosen Julien Temple to direct the film, because he thought that, being British, Temple could see L.A. from an alien's point of view. The studio balked at his choice. Refusing to dump Temple, Garnett cut the budget to $10 million and eventually found a way to finance the film independently, with the guarantee that it would be bought by the De Laurentis Entertainment Group (DEG) and distributed through Columbia Pictures.

The movie went forward, and Carrey won his role over scores of other actors who showed up for auditions. According to Temple, Carrey did by far the most engaging impression of an alien, and Julie Brown recalls getting excited by this outburst of weirdness and telling Temple: "Pick him, pick him!"

Once made, however, the picture sat on the shelf for more than a year. The problem: by then, DEG was a company in the process of being dismantled, and Columbia had a new regime trying to distance itself from decisions made by the old regime. Originally intended for release in the summer of 1988, *Earth Girls* was eventually distributed by Vestron Pictures a year later—nearly eight months after its well-received preview screening at the Toronto International Film Festival.

At the conspicuously otherworldly premiere in May 1989, about one thousand guests strolled across Hollywood Boulevard from Mann's Chinese Theater to the Spice nightclub for a party, where aliens costumed in fur jumpsuits amused the crowd, and those who weren't content to drink, talk and dance had a chance to get their hair ratted and sprayed into bouffants by studio-supplied hairdressers. Carrey and all his co-stars turned out for the event, and Julie Brown made her entrance climbing through the sunroof of her limo.

At this point there seemed little doubt that Carrey's career, which had seemed dormant a few years earlier, was on the rebound. Meanwhile, he was making important new friends. Among them was Steve Oedekerk, a future collaborator who befriended Carrey during his experimental period at the Comedy Store. And Judd Apatow, then a stand-up comic, later a movie director, instructed his manager, Jimmy Miller (brother of the comedian Dennis Miller), to take a look at Carrey. The result was that Carrey decided to leave Buddy Morra and David Steinberg after several years and hire Jimmy Miller and Eric Gold as his managers.

Perhaps the most important legacy of *Earth Girls Are Easy* for Jim was his friendship with Damon Wayans, who played Alien #3. Wayans came to the Comedy Store to catch Carrey's act and became one of Carrey's most appreciative fans. He expressed his

admiration by putting Jim's name on his very short list of performers no comedian would want to follow onstage. Backstage
after a show at the Comedy Store he told Carrey: "Hey man, you
are one of the angriest people I have ever seen."

Damon's brother, Keenen Ivory Wayans, was developing a new
TV series for the upstart Fox network featuring sketch comedy performed by a regular troupe, and Damon wanted Jim to audition for
the show. At first Jim said he wasn't crazy about the idea. TV was too
tame, too limiting, he felt. It wouldn't allow him to do what he did
best. Like Vegas, TV represented in his mind a road he didn't want
to go down—especially after his experience on *The Duck Factory*,
which was still a sore point five years after the show's demise.

Damon was persistent, and he arranged for Jim to attend a
screening of *I'm Gonna Git You Sucka*, a loosely structured parody of
black action movies that was a kind of calling card for the TV series
the Wayans clan was developing. Written and directed by Keenen
Ivory Wayans, it featured many talented, fresh black performers,
including three members of the Wayans family: Keenen, Damon
and their sister Kim.

There was no way Keenen could fail to take note of Jim. As
Carrey later told the story to columnist Rosie Levine of the
Toronto weekly paper *Now*, he walked up to Keenen all glassy-eyed
and told him what a great talent he was. Then Jim faked an assassi-
nation attempt, reaching into his coat as if he had a gun and point-
ing his fingers at Keenen's chest. By this point, Jim was jumping
around like a maniac screaming: "I took his life! I took a really talented life from this earth!"

Keenen turned to Damon and remarked: "This motherfucker is
crazy. We've got to get him on the show."

But to his chagrin, Jim still had to go through the audition like everybody else. Most of the performers on the show were going to be black, but there was a spot for one white guy, and this was a job that a small army of stand-up comics were competing for. Carrey's audition took the form of a performance at the Laugh Factory, a rival comedy club near the Comedy Store.

Jamie Masada, a slight, boyish former stand-up comic from Iran, had opened his two-hundred-seat club in 1979, when the comics were on strike at the Comedy Store. While Mitzi Shore was refusing to pay comedians, Masada offered a token fee. This started an intense rivalry that lasted for years. Comedians whose names appeared on the marquee at the Laugh Factory were not allowed to appear at the Comedy Store. But Carrey and other well-known performers could slip into the Laugh Factory without being advertised and still be booked by Mitzi. While the Comedy Store attracted a tourist trade, the Laugh Factory developed a loyal local following of repeat customers, and gradually Masada became someone the TV networks turned to for advice. Masada had a close association with the Wayans clan, and with Carrey's new managers. As Kelly Moran recalls, "Jim's reputation was growing, and he was known as a comedian's comedian. When Jim went on, his peers would stop whatever they were doing and just watch. They knew he was special; he was someone other comics could learn from. So by the time the deal was made for *In Living Color*, Keenen knew he had a goldmine."

By then Carrey had changed his mind about appearing on TV. He was convinced the show could be edgier than other TV material just because it was for Fox, which was trying to challenge the big three networks and wanted to add another winning series to go along with its cheeky hits *Married...With Children* and *The Simpsons*.

After he landed a contract to appear on the show, but before taping began, Jim had some distressing news from Canada. After years of deteriorating health, Kathleen Marie Carrey took a turn for the worse and died of kidney failure on October 5, 1989, at the age of sixty-one. She was buried in Burlington, less than a mile from the Aldershot neighborhood where the Carrey family had lived in the mid-1970s. The funeral arrangements were made by Jim's younger sister, Rita, who still lived in the Burlington area along with her husband, Al Fournier and their children. Kay's death provided the occasion for an intense family reunion. Now, besides having to confront his unresolved conflicting feelings about his mother, Jim would have the added anxiety of worrying about how Percy, devastated by the loss of his wife after more than forty years together, would fare on his own.

A few months before *In Living Color* went on the air, Kelly Moran spent a weekend near San Diego with Jim and a mutual friend, who (to Kelly's astonishment) had been lucky enough to book Jim for a one-night engagement at a local club. Jim was given to intense, serious discussions about life with a capital L. He talked a lot about his daughter, Jane, who had become the center of his universe, but seemed to avoid talking about Melissa. He had the air of a man who had found his voice at last and whose confidence in himself had been restored. Very aware that he was moving on to something big and exciting, he was also full of nostalgia for the chapter of his life that was now coming to a close. When the show was over and they were saying their goodbyes, Jim gave Kelly a parting hug. Years later Kelly would say: "It wasn't really me but the whole group I represented that he felt emotional about. I think Jim was embracing the memory of the Comedy Store."

fourteen

o o o o o

that Crazy White guy

WHEN *IN LIVING COLOR* made its debut on the Fox network in mid-April 1990, Jim Carrey finally achieved the breakthrough he had been lurching toward for years. Fox (controlled by Rupert Murdoch) had made its mark by being bolder than the three longer-established U.S. television networks. Its new weekly half-hour sketch revue showcased black comedy talent in a way that had never happened on prime-time TV (except for a show starring Richard Pryor that lasted little more than a month on NBC in 1977). This aggressively iconoclastic series was not only ethnically unique, it also stretched the boundaries of what was permissible on TV. The tone was set by the hip-hop theme music and Fly Girl dancers seguing into commercial breaks, but it wasn't merely packaging that gave the show its down-and-dirty appeal. Notwithstanding its prime-time Saturday time slot, *In Living Color* was sharper, edgier and hipper than any comedy series since *SCTV*. Yet, despite its boisterous, irreverent attitude, the show somehow managed to maintain such a genial spirit that it was hard to take offence.

Keenen Ivory Wayans—the creator, producer, head writer and host of the show—was aiming for the black audience, which had never before had its own satiric comedy show. Wayans had originally proposed an hour-long show—an African-American version of NBC's *Saturday Night Live*. But he agreed to compromise on the length of the show in exchange for creative freedom. At least one young Fox executive was convinced that there was a large TV audience desperately eager to find anything new and fresh on the air— and the show's success indicates he was right.

Besides Wayans, his brother Damon and his sister Kim, cast members included Tommy Davidson, David Alan Grier and T'Keyah Keymah. According to Keenen, the most important factor was that every member of his cast was hungry. (In his own case, what he seemed hungry for was prestige; the one off-putting aspect of the show was the self-serving welcoming speech from the boss at the start of every episode. This ritual was mercifully discontinued in later seasons.)

Carrey and actress Kelly Coffield immediately became known as the show's token whites. There was a certain irony in that, given Jim's experience with racial strife when he was a teenager working at the Titan Wheels factory. When asked about the racial politics of the show, he replied: "I don't think people see it as a black show or a white show, just a funny show." In any case, it wasn't the ethnic balance of the cast that provided the biggest challenge for Jim, it was the fact that he had little experience with sketch comedy, having come out of the quite different tradition of stand-up. But clearly this new way of working released a special force within him. To watch the explosive energy coming from Carrey on *In Living Color* is a jaw-dropping experience. It was as if this show offered the creative outlet for all the phenomenal talent Jim Carrey had been honing for years—as if everything up to this point had been a rehearsal for this opportunity.

Having been stymied so often in the past, Carrey was not going to make the mistake of failing to take advantage of this break. For the first time, Carrey was making a strong impact on a mass audience, with no need to hold anything back, and the experience gave him a buzz more gratifying than drugs or liquor. Carrey was a perfectionist who would keep colleagues working into the night if he thought a sketch needed one more take. Many of the sketches were taped before a live studio audience, and the audience feedback was a magical turn-on for him.

According to Paul Marr, a crew member on the show who met Carrey on the set during the first season, Jim was initially supposed to be just another performer in an ensemble cast. But within a few months it became obvious that Carrey had a special quality that made him stand out—even if his humor veered toward the juvenile. "Jim was like a non-stop force," Marr recalled. "He was so over-the-top and intense." It seemed obvious to Marr that this guy was destined to become the biggest comedy star of the next decade.

Predictably, the creative staff of the show encountered some interference from Fox network censors. According to Jim, about 20 percent of the material that emerged from the writing room was too demented to reach air—including one sketch about a right-to-life rally where a demonstrator performs with a finger-puppet fetus. But according to Carrey, most of the funniest stuff did get televised.

Often there was a chance to bring Carrey's gift for mimicry, developed in his old nightclub act of celebrity impressions, into the new (for him) format of sketch humor. On the very first show of the first season, Carrey gave a stunning display of rubber-faced virtuosity that also happened to be utterly hilarious. As game-show host Chuck Woolery, ringmaster of *The Love Connection*, he played the dating game with contestants Mike Tyson (Keenen Wayans) and Robin Givens (Kim Coles), grilling them on what presents they'd exchanged. Even now, tuning in to reruns of *In Living Color*, it's impossible to watch this skit without grinning, and it affords a marvelous glimpse of the talented impressions that first made Carrey a hit. Only here, he could also display his gift for acting, for comic timing and for interacting with other performers.

During the first season of *In Living Color*, Carrey worked in a number of other memorable impressions. Two of his best were Jerry Lewis, a twitchy nerd with an oddly angled neck making his telethon pitch for "Jerry's Kids," and silver-haired, self-satisfied Ted Turner wielding his scissors and savoring the opportunity to mutilate movie classics because he owns them. Perhaps his most viciously satiric creation was a spoof of the white rap singer Vanilla Ice, for which Jim was transformed into a spike-haired freak. And he was in top form playing Desi Arnaz as Ricky Ricardo in a cheerfully lewd version of *I Love Lucy* called *I Love Laquita*.

But the sketches that made Jim Carrey a hero in living rooms all over North America were not those showcasing his impressions of recognizable celebrities but the ones that featured weird fantasy creatures developed from Jim's imagination. During the first season, Jim introduced Vera de Milo—a grotesque female gymnast with pigtails, a tiny halter top, a husky voice and a reputed fondness for steroids. Preposterously demure, Vera responds to nasty rumors with the rhetorical question: "What's a girl to do?"

The character came out of something Jim dreamed up after a

chance encounter. "There was somebody I saw at Gold's Gym. It wasn't really Vera, it just gave me the idea. I'm like a gold miner, and every once in a while I find a little nugget. Sometimes a character begins with a spark of somebody's personality that I latch onto. Then I just pull it, stretch it, take it as far as I can. That's what this show is about. It's caricatures. Most of the time, it's about getting the laughs."

The lengths to which Carrey would go to get those laughs was astounding to those who worked closely with him. "He's a Renaissance man of comedy," said Tamara Rawitt, one of the show's producers. "There isn't anything he can't do. It's not a matter of 'What are we going to have him doing?' It's more a matter of 'What is he going to have us doing?' He's transcending the written material."

Without question, Carrey's best-loved creation was Fire Marshal Bill, which was introduced in early 1991, midway through the show's second season, and proved such a hit that it was brought back for ten more sketches over four seasons. This cartoonishly disfigured pyromaniac—with a missing upper lip, an ugly patch of scar tissue, one robotic eye and cords sticking out of his neck like unsightly cable wires—seems to have been pulled kicking and screaming out of Jim's own subconscious.

Like the Marx Brothers in *A Night at the Opera*, Fire Marshal Bill is an uproarious attack on pomposity, but the weirdness of the character is so extreme that he seems non-human—part *Road Runner* cartoon character, part scary monster from a cheesy horror movie. In Bill's earliest incarnation, Carrey developed the character in his stage act, without the benefit of makeup or special effects. "It started out as just a stupid thing I did in my act," Jim recalled. "Trying to shut the place down, I flew around the room telling the audience they were over the seating capacity."

Evolving over several years on TV, Fire Marshal Bill turned into his most astounding creation, bringing together in one brilliant package all the elements of Jim's talent—his rubber face, his instinct for mimicry, his knack for body contortion, and, in no small measure, the anger and pain he had avoided expressing for years.

"A lot of my characters have this thing where they think they're in control but they're not," Carrey explained. "I've worked in factories, and I've known people like that. They're funny but they're also sad."

Fire Marshal Bill is an officious man in uniform gone berserk, and it was by mocking authority figures that Carrey struck a nerve with the audience. There was also an element of payback for Jim, insofar as he was lampooning the management that used to infuriate him at Titan Wheels. And there may also have been a more affectionate trace of Percy, Jim's father, who used to leap about making a wild stab at crisis management while somehow managing to make everything worse.

Once he brought the character to TV, Carrey could invent endless variations, taking advantage of the medium's resources: makeup, special effects, set decoration. The audience couldn't get enough of this character, because whenever Fire Marshal Bill entered the scene, you could be sure mayhem was bound to ensue, but in inventive and entertaining ways.

Purporting to be a wise and cautious safety inspector, Fire Marshal Bill is actually a walking time bomb. He pops up in various potential trouble spots—a store, a classroom, a Christmas party, a cruise ship—and begins showing off his knowledge of how to prevent fires and explosions. "Let me show ya something" is his signature line. Getting carried away with his own spiel, he flaps around, spins out of control and invariably manages to blow up everything and everybody in sight. In one sketch, he sticks his hand into a meat-grinder; in another, he pulls a tooth out of his mouth with pliers. And when race riots turned the streets of L.A. into a war zone, Fire Marshal Bill seemed to have turned into a wicked send-up of notorious police chief Daryl Gates, screaming at one appalled observer: "To you it's a riot, madam, but to some people it's an insurance opportunity."

Of course, some people were dismayed by the Fire Marshal Bill phenomenon, including a group of fire marshals in New Jersey who went to a classroom to teach kids about fire safety and were caught by surprise when the kids laughed in their faces and shrieked: "Fire Marshal Bill!"

The more people tuned in to *In Living Color*, the more demand there was for Jim's stage act. That was all according to the career strategy of Jim's new managers, Jimmy Miller and Eric Gold. But it meant Jim was on the road a lot, performing all over North America. His grueling schedule exacted a toll: he was spending a lot of time away from Melissa and Jane. With more money coming in, the Carrey family had improved its standard of living, moving to the upscale Hancock Park section of L.A. But Melissa was having a hard time accepting not only Jim's absences but the fact that even when he was home, his mind was usually focused on work. And the more popular Jim became, the more he found himself being pursued through the aisles of supermarkets by teenagers who would say. "C'mon, man, do the face you do, do Fire Marshal Bill."

There was no question Jim was enchanted by Jane and devoted to her. He took her door to door on Halloween, daughter and father both wearing masks; the purpose of his was to pre-empt people from saying, "Hey, isn't that the guy from *In Living Color?*"

But there was a growing tension in the house. The more successful Jim became, the more Melissa began to sense their marriage was on shaky ground.

Because of the TV show, Jim was attracting a wider audience for his live appearances, and getting a response he wasn't used to. Before he became a familiar figure on TV, Jim would have to woo a comedy club audience and prove he deserved their applause. Once he became known for *In Living Color*, he was getting ovations before he had uttered a word. And people would call out requests for their favorite bits from the TV show—which was unsettling because it broke the rhythm of the act he planned to perform.

In the second season of the TV show, Jim began shaping his stage act to prepare for a cable television special. Both were called *Jim Carrey's Unnatural Act*. The TV special—produced by a company that Carrey formed, and dedicated to the memory of Kathleen Carrey (aka "Mommsie")—was taped in Toronto at Theatre Passe Muraille in front of a live audience, and it was telecast on the Showtime network starting in November 1991. Introduced by a group of dancers, Jim did a mixture of celebrity impressions, observational humor and patter about his troubled family. Sex burst onto the scene as Jim joked about the moment of ejaculation as "a mini-vacation from real life"; meanwhile his whole body seemed to be undergoing a weird set of orgasmic contortions. Tweaking one of his idols, he did a bit about James Stewart remaining calm and optimistic in the face of a nuclear holocaust. And perhaps the most startling bit was his material about his parents. "My mom could always smell something burning," Jim remarked. "I spent half my childhood feeling the wall for hot spots. Nine times out of ten it was my father. His favorite cigarette of the day was after dinner during his nap."

In retrospect, the special was not remembered as one of Jim's triumphs. Showtime executives considered it a letdown, and Jim (whose own company held rights to the show) withdrew it from circulation. That's why it is now unavailable to broadcasters and video stores.

Only a few months after the Showtime special reached the air, TV viewers were faced with a more startling departure from the Jim Carrey they thought they had come to know on *In Living Color*. Carrey appeared in a decidedly dramatic role in a movie made for the Fox network on the subject of a dysfunctional family.

The movie, *Doing Time on Maple Drive*, was directed by Ken Olin, best known as a star of the series *thirtysomething*. When Carrey auditioned for the role, Olin had no idea he was a well-known comedian.

Jim had to play a heavy scene between father and son. Olin was startled by Carrey's honest reading. "It was so sad," he remarked. The director came to the conclusion that Carrey had an understanding of the material based on personal experience. In the middle of the reading, Olin interrupted and said: "Who are you? I don't know anything about you."

Jim gave an understated, sorrowful performance as Tim, a young alcoholic—one of three unhappy siblings crushed by parental demands. Playing the difficult father, a restaurant owner and ex-military man, was James B. Sikking (best known for his role in *Hill Street Blues*). In his confrontation with his father, Jim as Tim says: "I resent the way you look down on me...And if I want a drink in the afternoon, I think I should have it. I don't have to explain it to you. I'm through explaining things to you. I've done my time on Maple Drive."

Making the film was an eye-opening experience for Jim. He

was gratified that his years of acting classes seemed to be paying off, and he enjoyed the novelty of not being under pressure to be funny. But the intensity was sometimes hard to take. "I'd go home some nights just devastated," he admitted, "because I had to be the miserable, vulnerable guy all day."

The film drew impressive ratings and three Emmy nominations, and Jim was given respectful reviews. In terms of Carrey's career, however, *Maple Drive* (telecast on March 16, 1992) would stick out as a one-of-a-kind curiosity—at least until *The Truman Show* came along.

In April, Jim got some shattering news. His friend and mentor Sam Kinison had been killed in a car accident at the age of thirty-eight. Many had predicted Sam's self-destructive behavior would end in disaster, but ironically he had cleaned up his life after realizing drugs and liquor were killing him. Sober and drug-free, Sam had just married Malika Souiri, a twenty-six-year-old dancer who appeared with him onstage and in music videos. They had just returned from their honeymoon in Hawaii and were driving in their Pontiac to a sold-out concert in Laughlin, Nevada. Sam was not wearing a seatbelt.

They were outside Needles, California (near the Nevada border), around 7:30 p.m. on a Friday evening when their car was struck by a Chevrolet pickup truck occupied by two male teens who were celebrating the weekend by drinking beer and driving too fast. Malika was knocked unconscious. At first, Sam—who walked out of the wreckage—seemed to have only minor cuts. But he had hit the windshield, sustaining massive head injuries. To a friend who was holding his bleeding head, Sam said: "But why?" Then, as if speaking to someone invisible, he said softly and sweetly: "Okay, Okay, Okay."

Jim attended the funeral along with many of the gang from the old days at the Comedy Store, including comedian Jimmy Shubert. It was hard for Sam's friends to accept that Sam could die just when he had made such a positive turnaround in his life. Jim adored Sam, saw him as the inspired devil of the comedy world, and had set out to earn his approval. It was Sam who had taken Jim under his wing and taught him not to be afraid to let the anger in his head come out onstage. It was because of Sam that Jim had shed his geeky side, which was just too clean and innocent to earn the respect of his peers. In many ways it was Sam who was responsible for the transformation from Jim Carrey I to Jim Carrey II.

All around Jim that year there were signs of unrest. Race riots and looting turned all of L.A. into a fear zone. On a more personal level, Jim was also troubled by signs that his marriage was coming apart. It was during this season of discontent that he received an offer to host the gala for the People's Comedy Festival in Toronto—organized by his old nemesis, Yuk-Yuk's owner Mark Breslin. To the surprise of some people, Jim decided to accept the offer. The gala was to be held in June at the John Bassett Theatre in the Metro Convention Centre and taped for broadcast in Canada. As part of the deal, Carrey stipulated that the show could not be broadcast in the United States. His job would be to do a certain amount of patter and introduce about a dozen comics. The fee was $40,000.

Near the end of the show, Breslin came onto the stage to do a tribute to Sam. He noted that he had just returned from L.A., where he'd attended a comedy benefit at which Whoopi Goldberg asked the audience for one minute's silence for Sam. But according to Breslin, Sam wouldn't appreciate silence; his life was about screaming. After demonstrating Sam's style of screaming—two shorts and a long—Breslin invited the audience to join in as homage to Sam. They did so with gusto.

As Breslin was leaving the stage, Carrey emerged from the wings and gave him a prolonged bear hug. It was an emotional moment for more than one reason. This was Jim's way of saying goodbye to Sam in a public way. And it was also his way of reconciling with Mark Breslin—the man who had once had him removed from the stage with a hook.

fIFTEEN

o o o o o

aCE IN THE hOLE

jIM CARREY did the best work of his career in the fourth season of *In Living Color*, which began in the fall of 1992 and ran through the spring of 1993. There were some cast changes, and it's debatable whether the show as a whole was as strong as it had been in previous seasons. But Carrey had emerged as a recognized star, and he was in phenomenal form week after week. He had obviously established a rapport with the show's writing team, creating sketches in which it seemed as if the zingers flowed effortlessly. Exuding confidence, Carrey had the glow of someone who was doing the work he was born to do, and knew it.

The 1992 U.S. presidential campaign provided him with two of his funniest characters. As Ross Perot, Carrey sported Dumbo ears and the rasping voice of a backwoods carnival barker. In the most wickedly funny of several Perot sketches, the candidate is doing a guest-speaker gig for the National Association for the Advancement of Colored People and using the occasion to sell the virtues of his

145

radical new economic system. He even spells it out on a black-board: S-L-A-V-E-R-Y.

Showing no favoritism, Carrey also skewered Bill Clinton as a curly-headed, promiscuous bumpkin, leading a team of cheerful nitwits known as the Capital Hillbillies while dancing and singing to a song called *Humpin' Around*. These were sharp examples of Carrey's talent for malicious satire—zeroing in with a killer instinct on a character's most reprehensible traits.

Fire Marshal Bill and Vera De Milo—well established as popular favorites—returned for a number of further adventures. And Carrey added gleeful impersonations of Geraldo Rivera, Jay Leno (with padded shoulders and a lisp) and one of his favorites from his early days at Yuk-Yuk's, the Amazing Kreskin.

A high point of the season, epitomizing Carrey's gloriously warped take on the media world, was his boisterous parody of "the Juiceman," who had turned juicing into a sacred cause. Carrey's version, the Juice Weasel, is a platinum-blond health-food-and-fit-ness guru (with bushy eyebrows) who struts around in a jogging suit while extolling the life-enhancing benefits of the concoctions he's whipping up before our eyes in his magic blending machine. Among the ingredients he zestfully feeds into the machine—and then drinks with enthusiasm—are eggshells, a bag of kitchen garbage, a potful of earth and a dead rat.

The darkest comedy Carrey has ever done is to be seen in a series of sketches called *The Dysfunctional Homeshow*, a nightmarish sitcom featuring Carrey as Grampa Jack McGee—an alcoholic nerd in horn-rimmed glasses and suspenders, stumbling around his kitchen endangering the neighborhood while trying to heat a can of pork and beans.

"I'm all dead inside," he proclaims almost boastfully. Jack is a truly bitter person, and a little frightening; the grim absurdity comes from seeing him placed in the banal context shared by the most familiar sitcoms about typical nice American families. It's like *Leave It to Beaver* rewritten by Eugene O'Neill—and then played for laughs. These sketches carry unsettling echoes of Jim's maternal grandparents, whom he used to mimic when he was a boy. Adding to the resonance for anyone familiar with his life story is that Carrey was clearly drawing on some of the anger of the socially downtrodden that he remembered from his painful days at the factory.

Inevitably, for some people in the TV audience, the *Dysfunctional Homeshow* sketches brought to mind the dramatic role Carrey had played the previous season in *Doing Time on Maple Drive*. You're not sure whether to gasp or laugh when Jack presides at the funeral of his mother (Kelly Coffield) and announces to the assembled mourners: "She was a sleazy leech, and we're all better off without her." When the allegedly dead woman is subjected to greedy relatives grasping for pieces of jewelry, she rises from her coffin uttering one of the great rhetorical questions of all time: "Can't a person slip into an alcoholic coma without being buried alive?"

Jim couldn't resist testing the boundaries of network taste one night when he was a guest on Arsenio Hall's TV talk show. Slipping into the role of Jack McGee, Carrey (who was completely sober) pretended to be drunk throughout his appearance, at one point calling Arsenio a "black bastard." For those who understood the joke, this made for great TV—but scores of outraged viewers who didn't get it wrote angry letters.

Carrey had been absent from movie screens for five years, except for an unbilled cameo appearance in *High Strung*, a minimalist and listless black comedy starring his friend Steve

Oedekerk, who was also the co-writer. (Playing a malignant apparition, Carrey briefly gave the proceedings a needed spark.) Yet he was determined not to take a movie role that wasn't right for him. Jim was reluctant to accept an offer from Morgan Creek Productions to star in a comedy about a pet detective named Ace Ventura—until he was told he could rewrite the script.

Ace Ventura, Pet Detective had a relatively low budget (by Hollywood standards) of less than $15 million, and it had been in development for five years. The original screenwriter, Jack Bernstein, conceived the story while watching a "Stupid Pet Tricks" segment on *Late Night With David Letterman*. Tom Shadyac, the director assigned to the project, had been hired on the basis of an amusing film called *Tom, Dick and Harry*, which he'd made in college. The script had been written with Rick Moranis in mind for the title role, but Moranis turned it down. A number of other actors were considered, including Judd Nelson, Alan Rickman and Whoopi Goldberg, before the deal was made with Carrey through his agent Nick Stevens (who at the time was best known for representing another young Canadian actor, Jason Priestley of *Beverly Hills 90210*). Working with Steve Oedekerk as "creative consultant," Carrey threw out most of the script except for the basic premise: Ace Ventura, pet detective, comes to the rescue when a finned creature named Snowflake—mascot of the Miami Dolphins football team—is kidnapped from its tank just before the Superbowl. The screenwriting credit was shared three ways: Carrey, Bernstein and Shadyac.

Just before flying to Miami to shoot the movie, Jim arranged a special evening with Melissa to celebrate their sixth anniversary, on March 28, 1993. He rented the ballroom of the swank Peninsula Hotel in Beverly Hills—and had just one table set. The two of them dined alone, and Jim serenaded Melissa with the help of his friend Phil Roy, who played with a hired jazz trio. Melissa was overwhelmed; she spent much of the evening in tears. In retrospect, the evening would loom as a sad milestone—their last celebration as a couple. The next day he left for Miami.

As Jim put it, looking back a year later on this turbulent time, it seemed like a Hollywood cliché: just as he was achieving the breakthrough he had always dreamed of in his career, his marriage was falling apart. In fact it had been troubled for a while. Audiences got a hint of the problem a year before the breakup when Jim included jokes about his marriage in his stage act.

"The other night I saw the devil," Jim began. "Of course I didn't tell my wife because I knew she'd only worry. But she's so perceptive I can't keep a secret. She accused me of never sharing my feelings. So I threw up in her face. That made me feel better."

While Jim was in Miami, his problems with Melissa escalated. Feeling insecure and abandoned, Melissa sensed that Jim was slipping away from her. She was suffering from anxiety and often made upsetting phone calls to Jim. Given the three-hour time difference between L.A. and Miami, Melissa's calls would sometimes come in what was, for Jim, the middle of the night, when he was trying to get a little sleep before an early-morning set call. Jim was so upset by his marital problems that one day, when they were about to film *Ace Ventura*'s climactic boathouse scene, Shadyac found Jim in tears in his trailer—and embarrassed about facing the crew in his fragile state.

When Jim came home during breaks in the filming, things did not go well. He was exhilarated about unleashing his full comic force on the big screen in a starring role for the first time. And he was unable to handle the old domesticity when he felt as if he'd just returned home after walking on the moon. "Living with me was like living with an astronaut," he remarked in hindsight. "When you're married, you've got to have time for this and that, and it was just impossible."

Shooting *Ace Ventura* was one of the most enjoyable experiences Jim had ever had; despite his private turmoil, he usually seemed to be in good spirits on the set, keeping his colleagues entertained and often bursting into uncontrollable laughter over some bit of comic business they were doing for the movie.

Melissa's attitude was determined: "You can't stop working on this marriage just because you're becoming a star. You must come home and put your feet back on the ground and take out the garbage like everyone else, or I can't be married to you."

The more successful Jim became, the more insecure Melissa felt. Right from the beginning of their courtship, Melissa and Jim had discussed the pitfalls of Hollywood marriages and vowed it would never happen to them. Now it was happening, and as far as Melissa was concerned there was one big reason: Jim was failing to live up to his end of the bargain. Their relationship was turning sour, and she felt she was being discarded, like one of his managers from the early days. Their circumstances had changed—the impoverished man she had married was now making millions of dollars—and neither seemed able to make the accommodations necessary to keep their marriage alive.

With euphemistic sarcasm, Melissa explained to a journalist that Jim wanted to enjoy stardom from the perspective of a single man. The more Melissa pressured Jim, the more she must have seemed like a reincarnation of his mother, who had provoked Jim's rage when, as a child, he had been lost in some creative reverie and she had interrupted to tell him it was time to wash his hands and clean up his room. Later on Melissa would admit: "I did a lot of yelling and screaming. I acted like a jerk. I should have just let go."

When *Ace Ventura* wrapped and Jim returned to L.A. in June, he moved into an apartment. Both Jim and Melissa began dating other people, but nothing was formalized, and everything was up in the air for several months until Jim filed for divorce. The official date of their separation would become an issue because, in June, Jim signed a deal to star in *The Mask* for $450,000, and under California law, divorcing couples are obliged to split fifty-fifty all assets at the time of their separation.

In October Jim called Melissa. "We have to talk," he said. "I've decided to go through with it"—meaning the divorce.

"Okay," she replied, trying to remain calm, "you do what you have to do." But she went into a deep depression, and she became even more resentful, speaking about Jim as if his behavior were a moral outrage. Before long, they were embroiled in a legal battle about the financial terms of the divorce. Jim offered a one-time-only settlement of $500,000 and $25,000 a month for alimony and child support. Melissa balked. The dispute went on for nearly two years before they reached a settlement.

Between filming *The Mask* and shooting twenty-six episodes for the fifth and (though he didn't know it at the time) final season of *In Living Color*, Jim had a frantic schedule. A New Line production, adapted from a comic book and directed by Charles Russell, *The Mask* had by far the most demanding special effects of any film Jim had ever been involved in, and he had to spend four hours daily in the makeup chair.

In a dispute with the Fox network, Keenen Ivory Wayans left *In Living Color* before the season started, leaving Jim as a conspicuous veteran in a cast full of new faces. One high point was a

series of sketches putting a new spin on *The Honeymooners.* Jamie
Leggett took Jackie Gleason's old role as bus driver Ralph Kramden, and Carrey was perfectly cast in Art Carney's old role as
Kramden's neighbor, Ed Norton. In one hilarious episode, Ralph
nervously awaits the arrival of a supervisor who happens to be
black, while Norton teaches him how to do the kind of dance he
thinks black people like to do.

Jim knew he had a lot riding on the reception of *Ace Ventura, Pet
Detective*, and he could hardly wait for the film's release in early
February 1994. Nobody was going to mistake *Ace* for a cinematic
masterpiece. It was just a goofy, childish spoof of a thriller, in
which Carrey is given an excuse to strut, cavort, flash his manic
grin and make funny faces while repeating certain phrases
("reeeeally" and "all-rightie, then") that had an air of likable silliness. The plot is empty-headed; Ace gets romantically entwined
with a football team executive (Courteney Cox) and has an ongoing feud with a nasty police lieutenant (Sean Young). Along the way
there are amusing parodies of *Saturday Night Fever* and *The Crying
Game*. Everything Carrey does in this movie is over the top, from
talking through his buttocks to dribbling birdseed from the corner
of his mouth.

As it turned out, this was exactly what audiences were craving
that winter. The theaters had been dominated for weeks by heavy
Oscar-worthy fare like *Schindler's List* and *Philadelphia*. California
had just come through an earthquake, and people in the east were
reeling from weeks of snowstorms. The first hint that the film was
going to be a hit came when audiences jammed theaters and
shrieked with pleasure at widespread previews the Saturday night
before the movie's opening.

On the other hand, the early reviews were dreadful. Siskel and

Ebert gave it two thumbs down, and critics used phrases like "lame," "surefire bomb" and "worst movie of the year."

On February 4, the day the movie opened in 1,600 theaters, Jim was in Chicago for a comedy concert on the college circuit, and he was worried. "Maybe the movie is a little stupid," he admitted to a journalist over lunch that day. Then he turned the situation into a comedy sketch, imagining how he would beg the college kids who turned out for his stage show: "Puh-leeee-ze see my movie!"

As it turned out, nobody had to be begged. That night, Carrey sat around with his team of managers and advisers waiting for the numbers to come in. "It was like election night," he joked afterward. Everyone was in a mood for celebration when word came that opening-day box office had exceeded all projections.

From Chicago, Jim flew to Atlanta for another stage appearance. He had invited his old friend Wayne Flemming to join him there. The two of them drove around checking *Ace* marquees and posters, and looking to see whether people were lining up for the movie. Amazingly, they were. Then Jim's publicist, Marleah Leslie, called with the news that not only was *Ace* shaping up as the weekend's box office winner, its three-day take was going to exceed $10 million.

"That's it, then," Wayne told Jim. "You're a big star now."

Staring out his hotel window, Jim replied: "I don't believe it."

By the second weekend, the movie had already grossed million. Counting the foreign box office and the video release, revenues eventually topped $100 million. Already Jim seemed living on another planet. A few days after *Ace* opened, he was d $7 million to star in *Dumb and Dumber*.

Jim the numbers were unfathomable. It reminded him of arly days in Toronto when he and his friends from Yuk-Yuk's would play Monopoly at 3:00 a.m. Jim rarely had fifty dollars to his name in those days, but to the group huddled around the board, he was transformed into a ruthless wheeler-dealer. Now, years later, becoming a hot property in the movie business, it all felt less real than one of those games. It was as if his career had become a matter of looking at the Monopoly board and saying as non-cha-lantly as possible to the other competitors: "Sure, I'll buy a hotel on Boardwalk."

SIXTEEN

o o o o o

fRED aSTAIRE ON aCID

IN *THE MASK*, Jim Carrey retroactively earned the huge success he had scored with *Ace Ventura, Pet Detective* by giving one of the most astonishing demonstrations of physical comedy prowess seen on the screen since Buster Keaton and Charles Chaplin hit their creative peaks in the silent era. You can't quite believe your eyes when Carrey morphs into a living cartoon with a lewd grin across his Day-Glo green face, creating delirious mayhem at a nightclub called the Coco Bongo in the fictitious Edge City. By some miracle, Carrey and his director, Charles Russell, had taken the magic of movies into a whole other dimension—with a little help from the special-effects team at Industrial Light and Magic (owned by George Lucas).

Turning a comic-book character into the live-action equivalent of a manic cartoon figure, Russell had the good fortune to have as his star the one performer in Hollywood who could pull it off. And Carrey had the good fortune to land a role that offered the ideal showcase for all his talents. No wonder *The Mask*—which cost

$20 million but looked as though it cost a lot more—was the number-one box-office hit in the summer of 1994. It delivered stylish, high-energy entertainment, and it was a true original—not quite like any movie made before or since.

New Line, an upstart independent production company that had made its money and its reputation with the *Nightmare on Elm Street* series and the *Teenage Mutant Ninja Turtle* movies, had bought the rights to the Dark Horse comic-book series. After a couple of years in development, however, there was still no viable script. The first drafts of the script had a somber quality, with a main character who seemed like a relative of Batman's nemesis, the Joker. No one could figure out quite what to do with it—until New Line's young president, Mike De Luca, approached Charles Russell, who had started his career with the king of B movies, Roger Corman, and gone on to direct the lively third instalment of the *Nightmare on Elm Street* series.

Russell suggested a lighter tone. "I wanted to set the story in a more colorful world," he explained, "to create the tone of old musical comedies. I saw the hero as a very musical character. He's a little hallucinogenic, a little 3-D, but there's a musical-comedy energy to everything he does."

Russell had been aware of Carrey since the mid-1980s. He saw Carrey's stand-up act at the Comedy Store while he was casting the Rodney Dangerfield picture *Back to School*. Carrey was briefly considered for the role of a professor, but Russell had decided Carrey was too young for the part and used Sam Kinison instead. By the time the script for *The Mask* was being written, Carrey had gone on to *In Living Color*. Russell thought Carrey would be perfect for the role—he'd had Jim's talents in mind when working on the script—but he didn't know whether he would be able to get him. He finally approached Carrey by sending him the first draft of the script.

After reading it, Carrey told Russell: "It seems as if it had been written for me."

Russell replied: "You're absolutely right. It *was* written for you."

The script had a great Jekyll and Hyde role that would allow Carrey to bounce his manic side off an alter ego who is amusingly repressed. Stanley Ipkiss is a timid Mr. Nice Guy with a dingy apartment and a dreary job as a loans officer at a bank. He's a Walter Mitty figure who allows himself to be taken outrageous advantage of—by the women he'd like to date, his boss at the bank, his neurotic landlady, a pesky police detective. His nerdiness is a wonderful tease; we know this sweet loser is going to turn into the kind of wild man we associate with Jim Carrey, and we can't wait for it to happen.

Everything in Stanley's life changes when he accidentally finds an ancient wooden Viking mask. When he tentatively tries it on, Stanley turns into the big operator he's always dreamed of being. Suddenly he is transformed into a charismatic fellow with a shiny lime-green face, a banana-yellow zoot suit and a big hat. This new, turned-on Stanley not only has superhero powers, he's a singing, dancing dynamo—"Fred Astaire on acid" as Carrey himself put it. And when Carrey swings into a Busby Berkeley song-and-dance extravaganza on the dance floor of the Coco Bongo, punctuated with a series of dazzling celebrity parodies—Clint Eastwood, Sally Field, Elvis Presley and Clark Gable, among others—moviegoers can be pardoned for feeling as if they're having a delirious pop epiphany.

At first Carrey was worried that the special effects might

cramp his style. Making the movie was a huge physical strain. Fortunately, the filming was all done in Los Angeles, allowing Carrey to go back and forth between The Mask and In Living Color. Though he started most days on The Mask with his four hours in the makeup chair, he was still ready to run wild once the camera was rolling, always inventing bits of comic business that weren't in the script. Russell was willing to let him improvise. This could have spelled trouble if the computer animators and visual effects producer Clint Goldman had insisted on sticking to the original plan, but they were willing to wing it.

"The element that makes certain stars exciting," explained Russell, "is a sense of danger, that anything can happen. It takes courage to be free in front of the camera, and Carrey is fearless. Jim was an elastic man to begin with. Now he is proud to have achieved a personal career goal by becoming a living cartoon."

Indeed, Carrey sashays around the Coco Bongo club with the verve of Bugs Bunny and the menace of the Wicked Witch of the West. His face turns into a leering parody of glee, and his own bag of body-contortion tricks is combined with amazing special effects. His eyeballs pop out of their sockets, his tongue slithers all over a nightclub table, and his heart leaps out of his body. He's as energized as a battery-operated toy, and completely insane. But it's Carrey's musicality that brings everything together and transports the audience to a new plateau of effervescent pleasure. You feel that the giddy celebration of Stanley's liberation from polite behavior wouldn't have found complete expression if he hadn't burst into song and dance. There are two triumphant numbers: one a romantic duet with co-star Cameron Diaz, the other a campy flamenco routine in which Carrey sports a Zorro hat.

The most amazing thing about The Mask was that Hollywood

had found a vehicle capable of showing off Carrey's talent with all cylinders firing at peak capacity. The question was whether anyone would ever be able to do it again. More than two months before opening on 2,700 screens across North America, *The Mask* was shown at the 1994 Cannes film festival, creating a stir and generating some hype.

It was while Jim was at Cannes promoting *The Mask* that word came through on *Batman Forever*. Warner Brothers had given up on Robin Williams, who had been wooed for the flashy comic role of the Riddler; Williams had not officially said no, but he was awaiting a rewrite, and was said to be reluctant to commit to the project. Now suddenly the part was being offered to Carrey, despite a potential scheduling conflict in the fall of 1994 if *In Living Color* were renewed for a sixth season. All this made for the hottest gossip of the season. "When I got the call in Cannes that they wanted me, I just couldn't believe it," Carrey later recalled.

Given the astounding success of *Ace Ventura*, the anticipated success of *The Mask* and his special appeal for young audiences, Carrey was considered a box office insurance policy. He was signed for $5 million. (This was less than he got for *Dumb and Dumber*, but it was a smaller role, and Carrey's deal, negotiated by his agent Nick Stevens, included a percentage of the loot from merchandising items featuring his character.)

The news of Carrey's signing caused a stir throughout the industry. The day after it was made public, Fox announced that it was canceling *In Living Color* after five seasons. Robin Williams was miffed that the part of the Riddler had been given to Carrey before he had officially turned it down. After extended negotiations, Michael Keaton (who had played Batman in the two previous movies) walked away from the project and was replaced by Val Kilmer.

Perhaps to get away from the frenzy surrounding him in North America, Jim took a holiday in Europe (where *Ace* had yet to open) and invited an old pal, songwriter Phil Roy, to join him. In Paris they were in a gallery when Phil fell in love with a huge sixteen-panel painting from the eighteenth century depicting Heaven and Hell. He bought it and shipped it home. When they were deciding where to hang it, Jim, suggesting a change of placement, said: "Move Heaven down here."

Phil remarked that the phrase would make a great song title, and before long the two of them were collaborating on a song called *Heaven Down Here*, which was eventually recorded, with considerable success, by the New Age jazz duo Tuck & Patti.

Jim's career was proceeding at a dizzying pace. After the release of *Ace Ventura, Pet Detective*, his life would never be the same. Public reaction to him changed. According to Jamie Masada, owner of the Laugh Factory, before *In Living Color*, audiences didn't react to Carrey when he walked onto the stage; they waited for him to prove he was funny. Once he was in a hit TV show, audiences gave him a warm welcome and requested their favorite characters. But after *Ace* came out, every appearance by Jim at the club provoked bedlam. "People would applaud and scream nonstop for three minutes as soon as he stepped onto the stage," said Masada.

Jim was now a highly eligible single guy, and he was enjoying some of the perks of fame, such as his newly acquired pale-blue '65 Thunderbird. But he was finding the dating game a horrifying experience. As he observed a year later: "I realized I could get laid every hour on the hour if I wanted to. But I quickly found out that I'm not the dog I thought it was possible for me to be. I really want someone to love."

He found someone—Lauren Holly, who happened to be co-starring with him in *Dumb and Dumber*. The movie was a comedy about two nitwits on the road together. Carrey plays a limo driver named Lloyd Christmas, who is so infatuated with one of his passengers that he's willing to drive all the way across the United States to return a briefcase full of cash she seems to have left behind. Jeff Daniels plays Lloyd's friend Harry, who has a hangdog expression and is even more stupid than Lloyd, if that's possible. And Lauren Holly plays Mary Swanson, whose lovely face launched this frantic expedition.

Jim immediately found Holly attractive. The daughter of two college professors, she had grown up in upstate New York, across Lake Ontario from Jim, enjoying a much more privileged upbringing. Before meeting Lauren, Jim, who was a high-school dropout, always felt intimidated by people who were well-educated. She was beautiful, fun-loving and available. (Holly was divorcing actor Danny Quinn, son of Anthony Quinn.)

At first, Lauren, best known for starring in the TV show *Picket Fences* and before that in the daytime serial *All My Children*, resisted the idea of getting involved with Jim. It seemed to her like an impossible cliché. But crew members noticed that the chairs of the two stars seemed to be getting closer and closer every day. And there were other telltale signs that made colleagues realize these two were smitten. Their on-screen kisses seemed a little more heartfelt than necessary, they were observed holding hands between takes, they were constantly visiting one another's trailers, and they laughed at one another's jokes with more than polite enthusiasm. But the most talked-about incident of the shoot was a to-the-death water-pistol duel Jim and Lauren waged in a hotel room.

In June, shooting was interrupted so that Jim could have surgery; his gall bladder had to be removed. While he was recovering, his old friend Wayne Flemming was summoned from Canada to spend time with him. There was an understanding between them that Wayne—who was still on the road doing the comedy circuit—would make himself available whenever Jim needed him. If that meant Wayne had to cancel engagements and lose income, Jim would make up any money he had to forfeit. To become famous, rich and successful inevitably leads to being surrounded by sycophants who tell you all day long how great you are. Wayne was not just an old pal Jim enjoyed horsing around with but a necessary connection to a grittier, less glamorous world than the one he had moved into. For Jim, maintaining his ties with Wayne—who had never become a big star and probably never would—was an essential kind of reality check. He knew he could ask Wayne a question and get an honest answer. And Wayne's loyalty was beyond question. Once, someone representing an American tabloid, hoping to get the lowdown on Jim, arrived at Wayne's door with a suitcase containing $30,000 in large bills; Wayne sent the guy away.

Soon after Jim's operation there was an awkward scene when Melissa came to Colorado for a visit. It was around this time that Jim's infatuation with Lauren was turning into a serious romance. Although Melissa's lawyers were negotiating the details of her divorce from Jim, she hadn't come to terms with it emotionally. Jim knew Melissa was flying in, but he was expecting a phone call to say she had arrived. Instead he was surprised by a knock at his hotel room door. Jim was inside with a few people—including Lauren. He was stunned to see Melissa, bearing gifts.

"I walked in and I knew," Melissa recalled later. "Everyone got real quiet. Jim got real nervous. And Lauren ran out of the room."

Holly hated the fact that she was being blamed for the collapse of Jim's marriage. "They keep calling me a home-wrecker," she complained. "I feel for Melissa, but they were completely apart when Jim and I met." In fact he had been on the loose for several months before she started dating him; she kidded him about that by calling him a "runaway train."

Commenting on the gossip about their relationship, Jim shrugged: "Everybody goes, 'Oh gosh, the leading lady and the leading man.' But if you're making movies, *that's* where you meet people."

Their relationship didn't upset Peter Farrelly, the director of *Dumb and Dumber*, who told *People* magazine: "They were *made* for each other."

It was, of course, impossible for them to have any privacy. Jim was now earning even more money than he had fantasized when he wrote himself that postdated check for $10 million. But he was learning that there was a big price to be paid. The level of Jim's fame had made it impossible for him to go to a restaurant or take Jane to Disneyland without being harassed by fans. Jim had bought a $4-million mansion in Brentwood two blocks from O.J. Simpson's house. (When ordering pizza he would explain: "Take a left at the bloody glove.") Often when Jim emerged from his house, fans would be waiting, begging him to do some of their favorite routines.

Even more problematic than unwanted attention from fans was the danger of being ambushed by the media. "You dumped the wife," the notorious Howard Stern said accusingly when Jim appeared on his radio show. "Who's that piece of ass you're with now?"

In late July, when *The Mask* opened in 2,700 theaters across North America and performed even more spectacularly at the box office than *Ace Ventura, Pet Detective*, any doubts about Carrey's popular appeal were laid to rest.

Soon after he finished shooting *Dumb and Dumber*, Jim got some distressing news. His beloved father, Percy—who had been increasingly confused and in failing health ever since the death of Kay five years earlier—died on September 13. By the time of his death, he looked gray and wasted, much older than his sixty-seven years.

Percy had been suffering from both lung cancer and Alzheimer's disease, and from the effects of chemotherapy. But when Jim was asked the cause of Percy's death, he answered: "Loneliness. He had already lost heart, and when my mother died, he deteriorated. He became manic-depressive. He was calling Rome to speak to the Pope. He was writing a book about me that made no sense."

Jim had never forgotten that it was Percy's own thwarted ambition to perform, and his tragic middle-age downfall, that had propelled his youngest child to the pinnacle of Hollywood. In a way, everything Jim had ever done was for Percy—to compete with Percy, to impress Percy, to satisfy Percy's ambition, to win Percy's approval, to make up for the tragic disappointments Percy had suffered. There was no one in the world toward whom Jim had more intense or more complex emotional ties.

Percy was buried next to Kay at the Gates of Heaven cemetery. The headstone had a heart-shaped hole in the stone along with a message that said: "Our hearts are empty without you."

Many of Jim's old friends from Yuk-Yuk's turned up for the funeral, along with members of the extended family. Absurdly, given the gravity of the occasion, Jim had autograph requests from people he was related to.

It rained that day, and as they were standing at the grave-side under umbrellas, Wayne could tell that Jim was holding back his tears.

"It's okay to cry now," he whispered in Jim's ear. "If your face gets wet nobody will be able to tell whether it's from crying or the rain."

Jim and Wayne both had a good cry.

The next couple of days became the occasion for a highly emotional gathering of the Carrey clan. Jim took Christian theology literally and seriously, and he worried about whether his parents would get into heaven. Afterward, it was said within the family that they had such a good wake they wouldn't mind if Percy died again.

rICH AND fAMOUS

dUMB AND DUMBER opened on December 16 and immediately became a huge hit. Almost unbelievably, Carrey had scored a hat trick, with three megahits released the same year. Written by director Peter Farrelly and his brother Bob (the film's producer), in collaboration with Bennett Yellin, the movie revels in low humor, with a lot of gags about bodily functions and physical discomfort. But it also happens to be smart, charming and very funny.

Dumb and Dumber came out six months after *Forrest Gump*, and for those who didn't join in the acclaim for *Gump*'s squishy, earnest lessons about the moral purity of dimwits, this lowbrow comedy came as a blessed antidote.

Exposing the chipped tooth he'd had since boyhood, and with monk's bangs and a bowl-shaped haircut, Carrey bears a strong resemblance to one of his childhood idols, Moe of the Three Stooges. He's in amazing, hyperkinetic form. His slapstick style is so graceful and precise it has the assurance of first-rate choreography. But he's not merely funny; he also takes exciting chances as an actor.

Yet many of the reviews were sneering, as if the title alone made the picture responsible for the "dumbing down" of North American culture. Consequently, this comedy, seen by millions of people in malls, was hardly noticed by the educated adult audience. However, it did win praise from the influential critic Pauline Kael, who had retired a few years earlier from *The New Yorker*. (Although she was no longer writing, people in the business still cared about her opinion.) "*Dumb and Dumber* is a very smart slapstick comedy," Kael said, "but a lot of people missed it because the title doesn't sound genteel, and the press tend to get upset by bathroom humor."

Indeed, *Dumb and Dumber* is not only irresistibly, boisterously funny, it's also touching. And Carrey delivers a sharper, more complex portrait of a dullard than the one that earned Tom Hanks an Oscar for *Gump*. There's a vulnerability and a courtliness underneath the manic comedy, and it's the co-existence of these qualities that makes Carrey's performance so engaging. He's playing a moron and getting as many laughs as possible, yet Carrey has the class not to be condescending. He lets us see that even a nitwit can be generous and good-hearted, and he catches the desperation and the poignancy in Lloyd's stupidity as well as the broad humor. Even when you're laughing at his Lloyd Christmas, you can't help feeling for the guy, and even rooting for him. And Jim was so serious about being true to his character that he refused to shoot a "happy ending" version in which Lloyd gets on a bus at the end. Jim insisted there was just no way Lloyd would ever get on that bus—and he didn't.

By the time *Dumb and Dumber* opened, Jim was deep into

Batman Forever. Warner Brothers had high expectations, based on the fact that two previous entries in the series, *Batman* (1989) and *Batman Returns* (1992)—both directed by Tim Burton—had a combined worldwide gross of $700 million. Still, the second *Batman* movie had not done as well as the first, and the studio's feeling was that something fresh was needed if a third movie was going to work.

Efforts were made to revitalize the franchise. For the third entry, Burton had stepped into the chair of executive producer and turned the directing reins over to Joel Schumacher. Besides Val Kilmer in the title role and Carrey as the Riddler, the cast featured Chris O'Donnell as Robin and Tommy Lee Jones as a disgruntled former district attorney known as Harvey (Two-Face) Dent.

By any standards, this was an extravagant production, with a budget hovering around $100 million, much of it to be spent on special effects and high-tech gadgetry. Carrey started preparing months in advance for his role as a brilliant technician named Ed Nygma who wants his employer, Bruce Wayne (aka Batman), to help bring his crackpot invention to the world's attention. When Bruce rejects the idea, Nygma becomes deeply resentful. To take revenge, he begins to transform himself into a villain with superpowers. That's when Jim Carrey emerges as the strutting, cane-twirling demon who torments Batman.

The movie set out to seduce audiences not only with comic-book mythology and star power but with lots of expensive toys. One of them was the Riddler's cane, which finds the Batcave's hidden entrance and unlocks a safe. Another was the Riddler's Lair. This pulsating, light-filled orb—80 feet high, 250 feet around and always in motion—had to be housed in a huge dome in Long Beach once used by Howard Hughes for his experimental aircraft.

There were a lot of big egos on the set, and things did not always go smoothly. Kilmer was said to be worried about being upstaged by Carrey and irritated by his bubbly manner. And one day Carrey's playful cane-twirling got a bit out of control, resulting in an unintended but painful smash to the testicles for Tommy Lee Jones.

Unfortunately, the hornet's-nest atmosphere of the set did not translate into excitement or energy on the big screen. Overproduced, noisy and vacuous, *Batman Forever* was remarkably lifeless and stale. It notably lacked any sign of the wit and visual ingenuity that Burton had brought to the earlier Batman movies. Schumacher's style was dark, clunky and graceless. Kilmer was rather dull as the Masked Crusader of Gotham City, and even Tommy Lee Jones, usually one of Hollywood's most reliably lively actors, looked as if he had no idea what he was doing there.

Despite all the disappointments, however, Carrey delivered. In the tradition of the entertaining villains who stole the first two movies—Jack Nicholson as the Joker and Michelle Pfeiffer as Catwoman—Carrey gave the picture's one enjoyable performance.

The Riddler was a role played in the 1960s TV series by one of Jim's childhood favorites, Frank Gorshin. Rather than imitate Gorshin, Carrey tried to go in another direction and give the part his own spin. As he did in *The Mask*, Carrey turned into a dancing, grinning dynamo with magic powers and a splash of green. But this time he was a satanic fiend with a skintight bodysuit, fire-engine-red brushcut and menacing voice. And if Schumacher kept Carrey's routine going a bit too long, it was understandable; this was one of the few elements in the movie that really worked.

Above all, it was fancy footwork and precise, snake-like body contortions that made for a mesmerizing performance. As Jack

Kroll observed in *Newsweek*, "Carrey cavorts like a nut Nijinsky."

Despite the picture's failings, Warner's huge marketing campaign drowned out the naysayers. Opening on a record 4,000 screens across North America, *Batman Forever* took its place as one of the highest-grossing movies of all time—not quite as popular as the 1989 *Batman* but more successful than the 1992 *Batman Returns*. The movie was a hit—albeit a stupefying one.

By now there could be no doubt that Jim Carrey had the Midas touch. In little more than a year he had shown his box-office clout with four of the top-grossing movies in Hollywood history. In addition all three of his 1994 movies were being turned into TV cartoon shows. For months it seemed impossible to find a glossy magazine that did not feature a personality piece about Jim. The ultimate exposure had come in March when he was one of three stars chosen to be interviewed by Barbara Walters in her annual special shown just before the Academy Awards telecast.

In late March, Jim left Los Angeles to start months of location shooting for *Ace Ventura: When Nature Calls*—the sequel to *Ace Ventura, Pet Detective*. The inevitable follow-up (once again a Morgan Creek production released by Warner Brothers) is supposedly set in Africa, but the picture was actually shot in Texas—at a privately owned animal reserve on a 15,000-acre ranch—and, later on, in South Carolina. The premise flows from Carrey's notion that Africa would be the place for an animal-lover like Ace to go. The script was written by Carrey's old Comedy Store pal Steve Oedekerk, who had also worked with him on rewriting the first *Ace*. But making this movie was not going to be easy.

Originally, the plans called for eighty days of shooting, but in a burst of cost-cutting, Morgan Creek squeezed that to sixty days. Chosen to direct the film was Tom DeCerchio, a screenwriter and director of commercials who would be making his feature debut. Right from the start, it was clear that Carrey and DeCerchio were not compatible. The production quickly fell behind. And tempers were flaring.

"It was a very rough schedule," says Malcolm Campbell, who signed on as film editor. "Every day you add to the shoot costs tons of money. What Jim needs from a director is a sense of confidence. He won't stop trying to improve some bit of business until someone says, 'You know what? I've got it.' In this case Jim just didn't feel sure the movie was getting done the way it should be."

After three weeks of shooting there was a terse announcement from Morgan Creek: "Tom DeCerchio has resigned as director due to creative differences. Steve Oedekerk will take over as director."

Asked whether it was true he had clashed with the director, Carrey said: "Tom and I didn't see eye to eye. We didn't mesh. It's a chemical thing, and sometimes it's nobody's fault, but you better get it right. It's not something to fuck around with. There's a lot on the line—a lot of money and people's reputations. It's my work, and I want it to be right."

Steve Oedekerk had gone to San Antonio, Texas, for what he thought was going to be a five-day visit to the set. Instead he wound up being on the road for months. This would be Oedekerk's directorial debut, but according to Malcolm Campbell he seemed to know exactly what he was doing. Still, the schedule kept changing, and recovering from its shaky start turned out to be a game of catch-up that was never won. Nobody seemed to know exactly how long the shoot was going to take. In the end, it took eighty-one days.

Carrey and Oedekerk enjoyed working together, but trying to duplicate the elements that made the first movie a hit was not a wonderful experience. Indeed, the summer of 1995 was not an easy time for Carrey. His divorce was turning into a tense struggle over money, as Jim balked at Melissa's demands for $7 million. The creative discomfort Jim was having with the second *Ace* movie was compounded by personal problems. Exhausted, he was afraid he was headed for a collapse. He couldn't make sense of the grief that would wash over him. At least once he found himself crying for no apparent reason. Then one day he had a breakthrough: he realized he was crying because he missed his parents. After years of playing the son who makes parental fantasies come true, that role had been snatched away from him.

During this troubled period, Jim's romance with Lauren Holly was certainly a plus, but they were both finding his fame foiled their attempts to enjoy life like an ordinary young couple. As a prominent TV actress, Lauren had learned how to handle being a celebrity, but the crazed reactions that Jim inspired were way beyond anything she had ever experienced. One night when she was visiting him in Texas, they took their chances and joined a crowd at a noisy bar in San Antonio. Before long, Jim had strange women jumping on his back. One of them asked Lauren: "Can I hug your boyfriend?"

She retorted: "Can I hug yours?"

In late July, there was a cover story in *Rolling Stone* that upset Jim. The article, by veteran journalist Fred Schruers, was an insightful and brilliantly written up-close look at Jim based on long sessions the two had in Texas on the set of *Ace 2*. Carrey had given Schruers more access than any other journalist, and the two had bonded. One of the things they talked about was Jim's messy divorce. Before filing the story, Schruers talked to Melissa, who gave her side of the story—in detail. Schruers then went on to suggest in print that it was wrongheaded of Carrey to resist Melissa's demand for a $7-million settlement. Somewhat naively, Jim felt betrayed by the article. That would be the last time he'd allow a journalist to get so close.

On November 2, Jim experienced one of the great highs of his life. That was the day he received Hollywood's ultimate honor—having his hand- and footprints immortalized in the cement on the Walk of Fame in front of Mann's Chinese Theater. His sisters and brother flew in for the occasion, and it was, among other things, an intense family occasion. Everyone felt sad about the absence of the two people who would have most enjoyed this day—Percy and Kay.

Jim's friend Clint Eastwood was on hand, along with Nicolas Cage, Wayne Flemming and hundreds of fans. Lauren Holly was at Jim's side. When it came time to put his hands in the wet cement, Jim added an inscription: "Merrily, merrily, merrily, merrily, . . ." He asked his daughter, Jane, eight years old at the time, to make the three dots at the end.

A few days later, Jim arrived at a Westwood movie theater for the premiere of *Ace Ventura: When Nature Calls* wearing a crimson tuxedo jacket. "I tried to keep him from wearing that ugly red jacket," sighed Lauren. Responding to cheers from his fans, Jim took a bow, let out a few moose calls and shouted a half-joking warning: "Don't worship me."

He had a point. This time box-office success was a foregone conclusion, but this crude sequel made *Ace Ventura, Pet Detective* look like *Citizen Kane*. The spirit of the sequel is true to the original. Once again Jim wears Hawaiian shirts and has his hair in a pompadour. And there's an amusing opening scene spoofing Sylvester Stallone in *Cliffhanger*, in which Jim (in lederhosen) is climbing the Himalayas to save a stranded raccoon. After that, the action moves to Africa. As for the plot, well, it involves African tribesmen and the search for a missing bat—which provides an excuse for Jim to ride an ostrich, feed an eaglet mouth to mouth, emerge from the anus of a mechanical rhinoceros, sing *Chitty Chitty Bang Bang* and utter the Tarzan cry through his butt. Unlike the original *Ace*, however, most of the shenanigans in this version feel desperate and forced. And this movie has a much nastier tone than its predecessor, perhaps an indication that Steve Oedekerk lacked Tom Shadyac's light touch.

Creatively, this picture represented a regression after Jim's work in *The Mask* and *Dumb and Dumber*. But all doubts were swept aside by the studio's elation over the box-office figures. On its first weekend in release, moviegoers shelled out a staggering $37.8 million to see *Ace Ventura: When Nature Calls* (a record for any movie opening on a non-holiday November weekend). And by the end of 1995, the picture had already grossed $100 million.

More than ever, Jim Carrey had established himself as king of the box office, with five hits in a row, the last four of which grossed more than $100 million each. Just a year earlier he had seemed like a wonderful fresh talent giving movies a needed jolt of energy. But by the end of 1995 he had appeared in two of the year's worst movies.

Nobody was going to admit it at the time, but a few years later Jim remarked: "I realized I couldn't spend my whole life doing *Ace Ventura*. The second *Ace* movie was kind of a letdown, because I was imitating myself. I was looking back at the first one and asking: 'What was the inspiration for this?' The spontaneity just wasn't there any more."

Surrounded by an entourage of business advisers who wanted bigger bucks above all, Carrey was coasting on the audience goodwill he had built up in previous movies. Getting high on the world's adulation, he had already become a prisoner of his own success. Whenever journalists asked him about his astronomical fees, Jim would say his career really wasn't about the money, it was about the work. That was starting to sound like a cynical line from one of his viciously satiric sketches on *In Living Color*.

Instead of using his commercial success to buy creative freedom, Carrey had allowed himself to become a crucial component of the most dismaying aspect of Hollywood—the cult of greed, and the noisy victory of massive marketing. In short, he was now embracing a show-business monster at least as vulgar and corrupt as the Las Vegas phenomenon he had rejected a decade earlier.

In June 1995, just when *Batman Forever* was about to open, Jim had signed a deal that was astronomical even by his standards. Columbia Pictures had offered him $20 million to play a weirdo in a black comedy called *The Cable Guy*. That was big news—the richest paycheck ever handed to a comedy star.

According to Jimmy Miller, his manager, the deal made Jim giddy and gleeful. "We really did it," Jim shrieked with delight. What he didn't perhaps fully realize was that he was being set up for a fall. That kind of money creates enormous pressure, and with so much money at stake, it's hard to justify taking the kind of artistic risks that Jim had been thriving on.

The $20-million deal was a turning point. Instead of being known as an upstart free spirit who had scored a triumph, Jim was turning into a voracious member of the Hollywood establishment—which inevitably made him the target for a lot of resentment. People were starting to look forward to the pleasure of watching Jim Carrey take a tumble.

TROUBLE TEMPORARY

THE CABLE GUY—shot in late 1995 and early 1996—was easily the darkest and most controversial movie of Jim Carrey's career. Conceived as a satire of stalker films such as *Cape Fear* and *The Hand That Rocks the Cradle*, the movie became a kind of therapy for Carrey, who had overdosed on manic comedy and was determined to try something different. He was operating out of the same need that had manifested itself in the mid-1980s, when he had thrown out an impressionist act that was drawing standing ovations because he didn't like where it was leading and he couldn't face doing it any longer.

Now, after less than two years of movie stardom, Jim had grown weary of the pressure to be a crowd-pleasing buffoon. The second *Ace Ventura* movie might have confirmed Carrey's position as king of the box office, but it also left Jim with an empty feeling. He had reached the point in his screen career, as he had earlier in his stage career, where he felt that giving the audience what they liked was a defeat, and the only challenge he could warm to was defying audience expectations, virtually daring people to walk out. It was as if Sam Kinison had come back from the grave to throw a chair at him and needle him about the evils of safe, easy success. He felt the need to raise the bar for himself, maybe even go through some form of penance.

As a desperate cable dork who calls himself Chip Douglas (a reference to the old TV series *My Three Sons*), Carrey juts out his jaw and talks with a lisp in a whiny little voice. "I could be your best friend or your worst enemy," he announces. He's a lonely guy who latches onto a mild-mannered yuppie architect (Matthew Broderick) and tries to bully him into a close friendship. At first he seems harmless and eccentric, even likable in an odd way. But just when the audience has settled in for a nice offbeat comedy, *The Cable Guy* gives them a jolt by turning into *Taxi Driver*. Chip's demons come out, and he pulls a series of scary, sadistic, violent stunts. It becomes clear that he's not just a bit creepy, he's a dangerous psychopath who is impossible to get rid of.

This might have come as a shock to people who thought of Carrey strictly as the infantile clown of the *Ace Ventura* movies, but it shouldn't have surprised anyone who had followed his work on *In Living Color*. There was a side of Jim that aspired to be taken seriously as an actor, and there was also a side of him that reveled in using comedy as a kind of social criticism. On *In Living Color*, Jim had enjoyed creating characters who had a humorous side but were also borderline sociopaths, acting out obsessions and rages while pretending to be in control. That's the kind of guy Fire Marshal Bill was, and Grampa Jack of *The Dysfunctional Homeshow*. But those were characters created for sketches of no more than ten minutes. *The Cable Guy* was an attempt to take a figure like that and build an entire movie around him.

That wasn't exactly what Lou Holtz Jr.—a prosecutor in the office of the Los Angeles County District Attorney, and the son of a well-known comedian—had in mind when he wrote his first screenplay. He thought of *The Cable* Guy as a light comedy about a needy, nerdy installer whose customers can't shake him. Holtz gave his script to two agents he knew, and he was elated when he got a call from Bernie Brillstein, one of Hollywood's most powerful talent managers. It was, according to Brillstein, a perfect vehicle for his client Chris Farley, the chubby young comedian who had recently made the transition from TV to feature films.

Columbia Pictures, which was looking for a comedy to release in the summer of 1996, bought the script, and Holtz had a series of meetings with Farley. But Columbia's plan to sign Farley was short-circuited when Mark Canton, the chairman of Columbia/TriStar Motion Picture Companies, learned that Carrey might be interested.

Once Carrey was signed, the nature of the material changed. Jim brought his own team to the project—including Judd Apatow, one of Jim's old pals from the Comedy Store. Apatow had worked as a writer for the HBO cable series *The Larry Sanders Show* and a couple of unsuccessful movies. He was signed as one of the producers, and was immediately put to work by Carrey rewriting the script. Ben Stiller, an actor who had made the Generation X movie *Reality Bites* (and later starred in the hit comedy *There's Something About Mary*), was signed to direct.

Carrey and his colleagues had a low opinion of Holtz's script, but they saw it as a fruitful taking-off point for something weirder, edgier and hipper. "The original script was basically a silly buddy comedy," Stiller claimed. What he, Carrey and Apatow wanted was a smart and dangerous send-up of psycho-thrillers like *Fatal*

Attraction. They went through four drafts of the screenplay trying to make it bleaker. And certainly nobody wound up complaining that the movie was too soft and conventional.

The shoot ended on March 4, the same day Jim was co-host of the American Film Institute's lifetime achievement award dinner in honor of Clint Eastwood at the Beverly Hills Hotel. Post-production on *The Cable Guy* had to be done in a rush so the picture could open three months later, and there was a lot of nervousness about it. The executive suite at Columbia/TriStar was a war zone, with studio chairman Mark Canton's job on the line. There were several different endings under consideration. And Apatow and Holtz were fighting it out through the Writers Guild of America for the screenwriting credit. (After the Guild ruled in favor of Holtz, Carrey and colleagues took a full-page ad in *Variety* thanking Apatow for his "wicked penmanship" and "invaluable creative contribution to the script.")

At the Academy Awards in late March, Jim performed a widely admired spoof of *Midnight Cowboy*, but Lauren Holly was not with him. Jim and Lauren had broken up. The split was a public event, and Jim was even willing to discuss it in the press. "Everything was great with Lauren except for my head," he explained. "My head was going: 'I'm not ready, and I don't want to hurt this person.' Although I have hurt her a little bit, I don't think it's as bad as it would have been down the road." He went on to explain that relationships "scare the hell of out of me. I just have this baggage."

In June, *The Cable Guy* opened to a remarkably hostile reception from the press. But it wasn't just the press that was antagonistic. Los Angeles is a showbiz town the way Detroit is a car-business town, and in June 1996, at almost any party you went to, the vibes could be picked up: it seemed as if the entire community was united by its antipathy to *The Cable Guy*.

"It's hard to find any movie executive outside Sony's Culver City studio gates that isn't rooting for the dark comedy to tank," said the *Los Angeles Times*.

"Everybody wants it to fail," gleefully explained a high-ranking executive from a rival studio.

It wasn't just this one movie. The Japanese-owned Sony Pictures Entertainment, parent company of Columbia/TriStar, was widely blamed for Hollywood's worst excesses. Over the past few years Sony had endured a stunning $2.7-billion write-off and an additional $510-million operating loss. Sony was commonly blamed for runaway inflation. Mark Canton was accused of single-handedly raising star salaries to new heights of insanity with the deal he gave Carrey on *The Cable Guy*—and a lot of people were hoping that a big flop would lead to Canton's ouster. (They wouldn't have to wait long.)

According to a report in the *Los Angeles Times*, Canton was furious about the bad press and tried to enlist Carrey to give interviews praising him for being courageous enough to take creative risks. Canton's wish was not granted. (Within a year Canton was sacked. When it became known that he'd collected a huge settlement, his boss, Alan Levine, took the rap and lost his job as president of Sony Pictures Entertainment.)

The mood at the premiere the second week of June was jittery. A crowd of 1,500 jammed Mann's Chinese Theater. Before the lights went down, Judd Apatow instructed the audience: "If you don't understand something, laugh anyway. It'll make the party afterward much better."

During the post-screening bash at the Hollywood Palladium,

Carrey seemed defensive. "I'm trying to do something that's a bit toned down," he explained. "It's about a guy who wants to have a friend. If people don't get it, if they don't understand, that's okay."

Apatow helpfully added: "It's like when Bob Dylan went electric."

The oft-repeated joke at the party was that, considering the movie's prospects at the box office, Columbia should consider changing the title to *The Straight-to-Cable Guy*.

The reviews were vicious. Janet Maslin of the *New York Times* described the movie as "a grim, sour Jim Carrey comedy" full of misanthropy and contempt. According to Maslin, the movie offered "the shocking spectacle of a volatile comic talent in free fall." The *Los Angeles Times* dismissed the movie as "a complete miscalculation."

Watching *The Cable Guy* on video today, one might wonder what all the acrimony was about. It probably seems like a better movie now than it did then. Its claustrophobic visual style works better on the small screen than the big screen. And if the movie is not ultimately satisfying, because the characters are sketchy and under-developed, it's still intriguing and provocative. There are some wonderfully memorable bits, like a scene in which Carrey grabs the microphone of a karaoke machine and begins singing his own nerdy version of Jefferson Airplane's *Somebody to Love*. At the very least, it's obvious that there was an interesting idea behind this movie, which is a lot more than you can say for most Hollywood blockbusters.

Even more striking than the negative reviews were the business stories suggesting that the movie was a commercial disaster and could be a big setback for both Sony and Carrey. One headline asked: "HAS JIM CARREY'S BUBBLE BURST?" The *New York Times* published a lengthy postmortem explaining "how a sure summer hit missed."

You might have thought someone had lost millions of dollars, but considering the circumstances, *The Cable Guy* did amazingly well. On its opening weekend it took in $20 million—far from a puny amount. And even with a steep drop the second weekend, it had still raked in close to $50 million by the end of June. Because of Carrey's astronomical salary, what looked like a small movie had cost $60 million; it needed to take in well over $100 million to break even. But despite many predictions of meltdowns, *The Cable Guy* did well enough overseas and in video to cover its inflated cost. The financial story about this movie had a happy ending, but few in Hollywood cared to hear it.

Since Carrey was about to start shooting his next movie, *Liar, Liar* (for which he was again being paid $20 million), there were rumors in Hollywood that Universal executives were calling for script revisions to make sure it didn't turn into another *Cable Guy* (Carrey, however, had to approve any script changes). The new prevailing wisdom was that if you were going to pay a bundle to Jim Carrey, you'd better make sure he was going to be funny; nobody wanted to take risks with that kind of money at stake.

Meanwhile there were also some script changes in Jim's personal life. In the spring of 1996, his romance with Lauren Holly, punctuated by a series of breakups and reconciliations, seemed to be over. But by July, the rift was mended. He was shooting *Liar, Liar* in Los Angeles; she was shooting *A Smile Like Yours* in San Francisco. Jim would often visit Lauren in San Francisco and gaze lovingly at her through the video monitor.

By this time, Jim had reached a divorce settlement with

Melissa. He gave her something close to the amount she had been seeking. Jim had finally realized that satisfying Melissa's demands was in his best interests. Eventually, she became part of the Carrey machine, working on script development. There would be no further public comment from Melissa about Jim's failings.

In September, Jim and Lauren were married on a hillside north of Malibu. Afterwards they invited ten friends to join them on a honeymoon trip to New York and London.

This was the second marriage for both Jim and Lauren, and both were determined not to repeat the mistakes of their first attempts. According to an interview Holly gave *USA Today*, she even pushed for a prenuptial agreement. As part of her divorce from Danny Quinn, she had to pay alimony—and it rankled. "It was very much an issue," she explained. "I did not want to be [financially] intertwined."

In November Jim and Lauren took a second honeymoon trip, which was meant to be considerably more private than the first. They chose an exclusive resort in Antigua which was a favorite of celebrities because it was considered an ultra-private getaway. However, they were hounded by a guest who seemed like a real-life version of the cable guy. At first the unidentified man and his companion simply engaged Jim in chat. But when this unwanted friend took out a video camera and began shooting his own home movie of the famous couple (it was their last day on the island), Jim lost his temper.

One of the other guests told the *New York Post* that Carrey went berserk and threw a pitcher of cold water at the offender—who wound up lying on the floor dripping wet.

Marleah Leslie, Carrey's publicist, offered a different version: "These people harassed Jim and Lauren repeatedly and continued to shoot video even after they had been asked politely—and repeatedly—to stop."

When the harassment continued, Carrey called the local police and asked to have his tormentor arrested. He more than anyone knew the dangers of making concessions to some weirdo who wants to be your new best friend.

LIFE aT THE top

WAS EVERY serious Jim Carrey movie doomed to fail? This was the question being asked at Paramount Pictures on Melrose Avenue in Hollywood. Paramount was producing *The Truman Show*, but the deal had been set before the debacle of *The Cable Guy*, and after the drubbing Carrey received for that decidedly unfunny venture, there was a lot of apprehension.

After returning from Antigua, Jim and Lauren rented an oceanfront mansion in Seaside, Florida, for the winter of 1996-97. This would be their temporary home while Jim was shooting *The Truman Show*. Carrey had agreed to do the movie two years earlier, while he was making the second *Ace Ventura*, with the provision that there would be a long delay while he fulfilled his commitments to do *The Cable Guy* and *Liar, Liar*.

The producer, Scott Rudin, had bought the script from Andrew Niccol, a screenwriter in New Zealand who specialized in paranoid fantasies. It was about an insurance adjuster named Truman Burbank who lives in a perfect house with a perfect wife—yet seems discontented. Eventually he discovers that everything is fake, that the people around him are actors performing for hidden cameras, and that he's the unwitting star of a hit TV series broadcast around the world.

Jim Carrey was Rudin's first choice to play the title role, and when the two met in the spring of 1995, Carrey said he could relate to the story: he had once taken family pictures to a photo shop only to have them turn up mysteriously in a newspaper. In fact, Carrey was so intrigued that he agreed to accept a fee of $12 million instead of his normal $20 million.

The names of many famous directors were mentioned— including Tim Burton, Brian De Palma and Steven Spielberg—but Rudin chose the Australian director Peter Weir. One of Weir's best films, *The Year of Living Dangerously*, had the combination of naturalism and poetic fantasy that Rudin felt the material needed.

Some observers were predicting conflicts between director and star. Carrey was known for seizing control of his films and bringing in his own script doctors; Weir was the kind of director who demanded absolute authority. But in fact their working relationship went smoothly. They agreed that Jim would not be involved in the shaping of the script, but that he would have some input into the development of Truman's character.

During the shoot, it was part of Jim's routine to ride a motorized skateboard around the huge garage of the rented mansion while he was practicing his lines. Often Lauren, every bit the star's adoring wife, would appear on set during the early days, but before the end of the *Truman* shoot she was off to Long Island to film *No Looking Back*, written and directed by Edward Burns.

Weir was nervous about the impact of the controversy over *Cable Guy*. "I'd heard about the lashing Jim had taken," he remarked later. "My fear was that he might have lost his confidence or become bitter." But this was not the first time Weir had worked with a manic, hyperactive comedy star; he had also directed Robin Williams in *The Dead Poets' Society*. And he had an effective way of reacting when he felt Jim was going over the top. One scene, for instance, showed Truman mowing his lawn. Jim added a silent comedy routine, dancing with the lawn mower. Instead of objecting, Weir calmly told Jim he needed one more take, and this time he wanted to try it without the comedy routine. Carrey was very obliging.

However, the *New York Daily News* ran a report suggesting that Carrey was taking himself too seriously. Apparently, at Jim's request, Paramount had issued edicts to crew members and extras forbidding everyone to use comedy catchphrases associated with Jim's goofy roles—such as "Smokin'!" or "Somebody stop me!" or "Alrighty then!"—within Jim's hearing. The extras, many of whom considered themselves Carrey fans, were said to be disappointed that they weren't even allowed to chat with the star.

More serious trouble developed toward the end of the three-month shoot when Dennis Hopper—who had been playing the role of a villainous TV executive—left the film, citing "creative differences." Less than a week later, Ed Harris arrived to replace Hopper. He had only days to prepare before going before the cameras.

The same week Hopper was dropped, Paramount sent a doctor to the set to give cast and crew members injections. The reason: a food-handler associated with the production had been diagnosed with hepatitis.

Meanwhile, there seemed to be an epidemic of the jitters back at Paramount. According to industry gossip, studio executives were braced for the worst after screening some of the footage. There were grim wisecracks about the folly of spending a fortune on a Jim Carrey movie that had no laughs, and *Truman* was being sarcastically referred to as a $60-million art film. Some pundits felt sure that Jim Carrey's career was in freefall. He had endured a painful fiasco the year before, and now there was a negative buzz concerning his next risky venture.

But Carrey's fortunes took a much-needed and very dramatic upturn when *Liar, Liar* was released just before Easter 1997—and turned into one of his biggest hits ever. For the first time, Carrey could be seen in a starring role playing a normal human being. He plays Fletcher Reede, an unscrupulous, mendacious, promiscuous and very successful lawyer, who is magically compelled to tell the truth for twenty-four hours. The idea wasn't original; a 1941 Bob Hope vehicle called *Nothing But the Truth* had the same premise. But for about half the picture, Carrey uses this shopworn plot as the taking-off point for some of the wildest, funniest riffs of the decade. It's a dazzling display of how an inspired performance can triumph over mediocre material.

The script, by Paul Guay and Stephen Mazur, is mostly a tired sitcom, but it has one clever, up-to-date twist: it seizes on widespread cynicism about lawyers. Fletcher isn't a bad guy, he's just a cheerfully sleazy opportunist with enough charm and good looks to get away with it. And while he is on friendly terms with his ex-wife, Audrey (Maura Tierney), and their five-year-old son, Max (Justin Cooper), it's clear why he was hopeless as a husband and father. He not only tells whoppers to win court cases for his clients and advance his own career, he even makes promises to his son and then reneges on them. After Fletcher fails to show up at Max's birthday party—because he's too busy having sex with a colleague who could help him win a promotion—Max sets the story in motion by making a secret wish: that Fletcher be forced to tell the truth for an entire day.

This could have been a groaner, but director Tom Shadyac—who was at the helm of *Ace Ventura, Pet Detective* and the 1996 Eddie Murphy remake of *The Nutty Professor*—knew exactly how to unleash the Dr. Jekyll side of his star. In a scene so deliciously raucous that it justifies sitting through the boring parts, Fletcher goes to a board meeting where he makes what seems at first like the hilariously disastrous gaffe of telling each of the senior lawyers exactly what he thinks of them. There's a stunned silence—until the first victim explodes with laughter. Then everybody explodes with laughter, and Fletcher fires insults around the room in response to a sudden appetite for outrageous abuse. A stuffy board meeting turns into the wildest celebrity roast of all time.

In court, representing a tacky adulteress (Jennifer Tilly), Fletcher tries frantically to lie, but he is a man possessed, and the words won't come out. When he asks leading questions, the truth patrol within him won't let him get away with it, and he objects to his own questions. Carrey's comic portrait of a man at war with himself reaches some sort of insane peak when he goes into the men's room and beats himself up—which could be a subversive comment on the notoriously unfunny washroom violence in *The Cable Guy*.

Unfortunately, the movie does not stay on this sublimely funny level. Instead, it stops dead in its tracks and attempts to teach earnest lessons about the importance of being a good father. The new, wiser, more responsible Fletcher turns out to be a whole lot less funny, and also less likable, than the reprehensible version. Truth to tell, Fletcher becomes an insufferably self-righteous windbag. In its last half hour, *Liar, Liar* gets as hopelessly sappy as Frank Capra at his most maudlin, and there's not much you can do except hide under your seat until the shameless message-mongering is over. Even an elaborate physical stunt—Fletcher riding a motorized stairway down a runway to stop a plane from leaving with his wife and son—falls flat because of sloppy execution.

And at the very end of *Liar, Liar*, the movie gets more shamelessly cute than you might have thought possible, when Max makes another birthday wish—and his estranged parents are suddenly locked in a passionate kiss.

"Max," asks our chastened hero suspiciously, "did you make a wish for your Mom and I to get back together?" What he should have said, if only the writers had been a bit more at ease with the English language, was "Did you make a wish for your Mom and *me* to get back together?" Which leaves open the possibility for a brilliant sequel about a character who is prohibited for twenty-four hours from making grammatical errors.

Still, as the final credits roll, Shadyac adds a needed punchline with some goofy outtakes of comedy routines that went awry. You can almost erase the mushy stuff from your mind and leave the theater grinning over Carrey's comic high points.

At the box office, *Liar, Liar* exceeded all expectations, taking in $32 million on its first weekend—the highest March-opening total in movie history. It eventually went on to take in a mind-boggling $179 million in North America alone.

Once again, a surge in Carrey's career coincided with the collapse of a marriage. In May, Carrey moved out of the Brentwood house he shared with Holly and into the Bel-Air Hotel. One night

Jim caused a bit of a stir by turning up alone at the hotel bar, asking the pianist to play some of his favorite songs. Jim even sang a couple of tunes from *The Phantom of the Opera*. Oprah Winfrey, who happened to be at the bar, joined Jim for a while and sang along. *Newsday* columnist Liz Smith quoted an anonymous insider as saying: "The marriage died the first weekend *Liar, Liar* did so well. Lauren is a very ambitious, competitive woman. And Jim's not easy to live with either. No comic is."

Lauren was conspicuously absent on the first Sunday of June when Jim picked up two awards for *The Cable Guy* at the MTV Awards in a ceremony hosted by Mike Myers. When he won the award for Best Villain, Jim jumped out of his seat and ran screaming through the audience like a lunatic. At the podium, he thanked executives at Sony Pictures—who by then had been fired—and said he hoped they had all found new jobs. Then Carrey remarked: "I'll remember this not as an award but as undeniable proof that I am a badass motherfucker." Later in the evening, he won another award for best comedy performance.

Holly appeared in public on several occasions with Edward Burns, who had directed her in *No Looking Back*. And in late July, only ten months after their wedding, she filed for divorce in Los Angeles Superior Court, citing "irreconcilable differences." According to court documents, they had separated on June 25. Surprisingly, since she had referred in press interviews to a prenuptial agreement, Holly was seeking spousal support and legal fees. Meanwhile, Jim and Lauren issued identical statements saying that they wished only the best for one another.

Jim had moved back into the Brentwood house. In October, Lauren bought a house in Beverly Hills for just under $2 million, featuring spectacular views, a pool, a spa and a fountain.

Throughout the summer of 1997 the trade press was abuzz with rumors of deals for future Carrey movies. At one point his agent was negotiating with Warner Brothers about a new *Superman* movie, to be directed by Tim Burton. Nicolas Cage was to play the title role, with Carrey cast as Brainiac, an evil android trying to destroy the world. But the deal evaporated, and the movie was back-burnered.

Plans for a remake of *The Secret Life of Walter Mitty* reached a more serious stage. This was to be the second movie based on the James Thurber story about a wimp who daydreams about being a great hero (in the lackluster 1947 version, the part was played by Danny Kaye). The new film was going to be produced by New Line and directed by Ron Howard. But the project was stalled by script trouble, and Carrey moved on to other projects.

Carrey was very enthusiastic about starring in another remake, *The Incredible Mr. Limpet.* The 1964 original, starring Don Knotts as a mild-mannered navy man who becomes a fish, was a favorite of Jim's. The film was going to be produced by Warner Brothers, and, at Jim's request, his friend Steve Oedekerk was being hired to rewrite the script and direct the picture.

In December, Jim caused a sensation at the VH1 Fashion Awards in New York's Madison Square Garden when he sauntered down the catwalk eating an apple and wearing only a fig leaf—a very large fig leaf. The hosts for the event were Ashley Judd and Harry Connick Jr. Jim's role was to introduce the Rolling Stones, who were headlining the evening. "This is where fashion began," Carrey told the howling crowd. "This fig leaf was originally modeled by Adam in the Garden of Eden."

At Christmas, Jim went to Toronto for a reunion with his family. As usual, he stayed with Rita, the younger of his two sisters (just a year older than Jim), who lived near Waterdown (southwest of Burlington) with her husband, Al Fournier, and their three teenage sons. For some time Rita had been working for Burlington Transit, driving buses, helping in the office and doing radio dispatch.

Since the death of their parents, Jim had made a point of staying in close touch with his three siblings. His visits presented certain logistical problems, though: he had to be accompanied by a bodyguard; and outings to restaurants such as Centro, one of Toronto's most fashionable Italian spots, inevitably brought a certain amount of attention.

Buying a Christmas present for Jim was a challenge for Rita, but she settled on a table-hockey game. Jim seemed to get a kick out of that; they sat around playing the game while Jim imitated a play-by-play announcer: "There's Dave Keon, over to Sergei Grinkov . . ."

For New Year's Eve, Jim rented a suite at the elegant King Edward Hotel large enough to accommodate his siblings, their families and a few special friends, including Wayne Flemming. Toronto jazz musician Mike Welsman was hired to play the piano. Adding to the festive mood was the fact that Jim's older sister, Pat, who had been divorced for several years, was about to get remarried.

The material chosen for the occasion included songs by Elton John, Supertramp, Peter Gabriel and Creedence Clearwater Revival. Welsman was a little worried that he might be playing to the drapes and furniture, but the Carrey family turned out to be spirited collaborators. Rita was an accomplished singer who sometimes performed at a Waterdown club, and one of Jim's nephews was eager to jam with Welsman. It was a cozy evening, filled with talking, singing and laughing. Except for the luxurious surroundings, and the conspicuous absence of Percy and Kay, it was very much like a Carrey family gathering in the old days.

For Jim, 1997 had been a year of spectacular extremes, both personally and professionally—and 1998 would hold a few surprises as well.

Shooting

For the moon

It SEEMED unthinkable to ask Hollywood's hottest, highest-paid actors to audition for a part. Indeed, many of the most prominent stars won't even read a script until a firm offer has been made. But Miloš Forman got away with it. Forman—the Czech emigré who directed *One Flew Over the Cuckoo's Nest*, *Amadeus* and *The People vs. Larry Flynt*—was casting a role coveted by a number of leading actors. It was the part of Andy Kaufman, the enigmatic comedian from Great Neck, New York, who loved to blur the distinction between what was real and what was an act, creating so much confusion along the way that when he died of lung cancer in 1984 at age thirty-five, some people thought it was a hoax.

Years after his death, Kaufman—known to millions of TV viewers through *Saturday Night Live* and *Taxi*—looms as something of a legend. Certainly no name is hotter in the specialized category of dead comedians. What made him unique was the way he combined elements of avant-garde theater with the conventions of stand-up comedy. On at least one occasion, he took his entire audience out for ice cream, and on another his performance was a reading of *The Great Gatsby* in its entirety. He had a knowing little smile and a loony, faraway "nobody's home" look in his eyes that was reminiscent of Harpo Marx. But with Kaufman, you could never quite be sure how you were meant to take what you were watching. And maybe it's this ambiguous quality, combined with his early death, that accounts for his weird posthumous mystique.

In perhaps the most celebrated/notorious incident of his life, Kaufman clashed with a brutal and vindictive professional wrestler named Jerry Lawler. After wrestling with women on many occasions (one of his most disconcerting stunts) and declaring himself "inter-gender wrestling champion," Kaufman accepted a challenge from the pro. The match took place in Memphis in 1982 and ended when Kaufman was taken to hospital on a stretcher. Lawler felt Kaufman was trying to ridicule him, and he responded the only way he knew how.

After Kaufman got out of hospital, he and Lawler met for a much-talked-about confrontation on David Letterman's old late-night NBC show. At the suggestion that his injury might be fake, Andy (who was still wearing a neck brace) began delivering an emotional tirade. In the middle of it, having been insulted by Kaufman, Lawler whacked him across the face. Swearing profusely, Andy threw a cup of coffee in his tormentor's face and walked off the show. The anger seemed genuine, but with Kaufman you could never be sure. Was this for real, or was it another piece of invention? Kaufman challenged anyone who thought his injuries were fake to check with the hospital and look at the X-rays. He also threatened to sue NBC for $200 million.

As Letterman once remarked: "Sometimes when you look Andy in the eyes, you get the sense somebody else is driving." Jay

Leno put it another way: "With Andy you were never sure whom you were talking to."

Man on the Moon (the title comes from a song about Kaufman by REM) created excitement as soon as the project was announced. The movie was being co-produced by Universal Studios and Jersey Films, a company controlled by Kaufman's former TV co-star Danny DeVito—who was going to portray Kaufman's manager, George Shapiro. The script was by Larry Karaszewski and Scott Alexander, who had worked with Forman on *The People vs. Larry Flynt*, and the movie was to be shot in the summer of 1998. Forman sent videos of Kaufman to the actors on his shortlist, asking them to send audition videos back to him. While Forman's request was unorthodox, if not outrageous, he had an explanation: it would be less trouble for the actors to do an audition tape than attend meetings. Jim Carrey was only one of the big names being mentioned initially as possibilities for the role. The list also included Carrey's friend Nicolas Cage, Edward Norton, John Cusack, Kevin Spacey and Gary Oldman.

Carrey was a fan of Kaufman's and had been influenced by him during his stand-up days, but since he seemed to come out of a completely different comedy tradition, Jim didn't appear at first to have the inside track. Cage seemed to be the early favorite. But Cage was offended by the request to submit an audition tape, and more or less took himself out of the running.

Carrey, too, could have taken the position that it would be beneath him to audition, but he was intrigued by the part. So, as he told Oprah Winfrey later, he decided to make the audition tape and submit it if it turned out well; if he hadn't liked the way it turned out, Carrey explained jokingly, he would have just said it was beneath him to audition.

Of course, anyone who knew Carrey's talent for doing impressions and had seen his work on *In Living Color* might have predicted the outcome. All the candidates were assured the tapes would be absolutely confidential. Nevertheless, details were leaked about Carrey's audition, which was shot in the living room of his Brentwood home. Dressed in a peach-colored tuxedo, Jim as Andy recreated some of Kaufman's best-remembered characters—including Las Vegas lounge lizard Tony Clifton, the bad-guy wrestler and Foreign Man (precursor to Latka, the character Andy played on *Taxi*). Carrey even managed to use the bongo drums actually owned by Kaufman.

Edward Norton's audition tape was also said to be great—but a runner-up to Carrey's. After viewing all the tapes, it was immediately clear to Forman who was going to play Andy Kaufman. And to make sure he was making the right decision, he arranged a private screening of *The Truman Show*. In early March, Carrey was signed for the part.

After a long series of delays, *The Truman Show* finally had a release date: the first weekend of June. Originally the movie—shot in early 1997—was supposed to be released in August of that year. Then it was rescheduled for November, and again for February 1998. The delays provided endless fuel for negative gossip. Paramount was nervous, especially after exhibitors at a Las Vegas trade show reacted to early glimpses of scenes with complete bewilderment. It was speculated that this was going to be *Cable Guy II*, and that Paramount should be braced for a meltdown.

Before the movie's release, Carrey made two hugely successful appearances on television. One was a full hour devoted to him on *Oprah*. Jim and Oprah Winfrey made a wonderfully engaging team; they compared notes on intimate relationships and did an anything-you-can-do-I-can-do-better routine about which of them had endured the more impoverished childhood.

Carrey's other attention-grabbing TV appearance was on a special hour-long final episode of *The Larry Sanders Show* on HBO. Carrey demonstrated his talent for sketch comedy, playing "Jim Carrey" as a wildly sycophantic celebrity guest who turns cold and nasty as soon as the show leaves the air. This was easily the most hilarious part of Larry's star-studded swan song. It was also a great promotion for *The Truman Show.*

On June 1, a new and more dignified Jim Carrey stepped out of his limo at the premiere of *The Truman Show* in Los Angeles. Two facts were immediately apparent: one, Jim, keeping a straight face, was declining to goof around; and two, Lauren Holly was at his side.

Their much-publicized divorce notwithstanding, this on-and-off romance seemed to be very much on again. In mid-March, just before the Academy Awards, Hollywood gossip columnists had enjoyed a feeding frenzy when Carrey and Holly were spotted together on several occasions. Their second-time-around courtship progressed to the point that together they rented a six-bedroom Malibu beachhouse for the summer from Sting, the British pop singer. But when reporters at the *Truman* premiere asked about a possible remarriage, Jim and Lauren replied in robot-like unison: "Access denied."

The publicity buildup for *The Truman Show* had been brilliantly managed. Despite pre-release jitters that it could turn out to be a debacle, this movie attracted a glowing, positively reverential press response. It scored a first in one respect: it became the first Jim Carrey movie to be marketed on the basis of reviews. The ad campaign was built around a quote from a rave notice in *Esquire* by

David Thomson, who had been given a screening months in advance. His verdict: "*The Truman Show* is the movie of the decade." It was the kind of over-the-top pronouncement that seemed calculated to raise the critic's profile—and in fact, Paramount plastered that phrase in huge type all over double-page color ads for weeks before the movie opened. The strategy succeeded in setting the tone for a media blitz, which included a cover story in *Time* magazine. Everyone seemed to be impressed by the fact that Jim Carrey had given up infantile shenanigans and turned into a serious actor, sort of like his boyhood hero James Stewart in *It's a Wonderful Life*.

It can seem like a form of deprivation to see Jim Carrey in a movie where he's hardly allowed to be funny, and it's alarming to think he could be following in the footsteps of Robin Williams, whose career has taken a horrifying turn in recent years. (Not content with being one of the funniest people on the planet, Williams has become insufferably inspirational and sentimental.) But luckily Carrey doesn't come across as pious. Instead he gives a restrained, low-key performance as the hero/victim Truman Burbank—a man whose entire life is an elaborate contrivance—and he makes the movie seem almost plausible.

The Truman Show is far from a great movie, but it's tolerable: you can go along for the ride even if you never quite buy it. It's partly carried by outstanding production design and a compelling performance from Ed Harris as Christof, the calculating, malevolent schemer who has substituted trained actors for all the people in Truman's life, including his wife and mother. Christof tries to stifle Truman's yearning for something authentic, but he hadn't counted on the surprise reappearance of a disaffected actor who used to play Truman's father. The audience is expected to cheer

Truman's rebellion, and it's assumed we will accept the premise without question. But *The Truman Show* doesn't bear scrutinizing. This is a film of ideas whose ideas are halfbaked. The irony is that Peter Weir pretty much programs and controls his audience as relentlessly and single-mindedly as Christof.

To the extent to which the movie is subliminally affecting, it's probably because Carrey brings a quality to the material that a lot of people could relate to—the quiet desperation of the reasonably good-looking, healthy, normal-seeming person who seems to be living a satisfactory life, yet has the nagging feeling that daily reality has turned into a make-believe game, that something has gone deeply and terribly wrong, and that the malaise cannot be fixed by any other means except a complete break with the past. Carrey even manages to slip in a few traces of personality that help mitigate the gloom.

If Carrey seems right for this role, it may be through the legacy of his desperately needy childhood; he knows in his bones how to behave as if everything is fine while suggesting that at a deeper level he understands something has gone hideously wrong. Contrived and strained as *The Truman Show*'s setup may be, Carrey delivered a haunting, compelling performance.

Even if the movie wasn't a lot of fun to sit through, people were intrigued enough by its strained seriousness to jam malls all over North America. Imagine: Jim Carrey behaving like a grown-up, and playing a quietly unhappy character. It was the sort of thing everyone had to have an opinion about. Consequently *Truman* raked in an amazing $31 million at the box office in its first weekend and was well on its way to being one of the few big hits of the summer. Carrey now seemed more formidable than ever. It was one thing to score a box-office success with a broad popular comedy; it was quite another to pull in more than $100 million with an offbeat parable that would probably have died commercially if anyone else had played the title role.

Forman began filming *Man on the Moon* in late July in Los Angeles. Several members of the *Taxi* ensemble—Judd Hirsch, Marilu Henner, Jeff Conaway and Carol Kane—were hired to play themselves. Also cast as himself was Jerry Lawler. Almost immediately anecdotes began making the rounds about Jim's bizarre transformation. He was living the part, behaving like Andy twenty-four hours a day. He demanded two trailers—one for Andy and one for Tony Clifton, Andy's alter ego. He even asked crew members to call him Andy, not Jim. And Carrey adopted certain odd habits that would have been typical of Kaufman, such as serving ice cream to everyone and dragging a replica of Howdy Doody around the set. At certain times, when he was portraying Tony—who had supposedly been fired from *Taxi*—Jim would become impossibly obnoxious, baiting other members of the *Taxi* cast.

Tensions came to a head in late September during the filming of the wrestling sequence. Between takes, Jim stayed in character. He even spat in Lawler's face when the cameras weren't rolling. Lawler reacted furiously and ran across the ring to pull Jim's hair and grab his neck. There was a trickle of blood from the right side of Jim's face, and security guards rushed in to separate the combatants. At first, witnesses feared that Carrey had been seriously injured, but he was released from hospital after tests and returned to the set the next day—wearing a neck brace.

Meanwhile, Lauren Holly was no longer in Jim's life. This time they had come to a clear understanding that the parting was permanent. They would always care for one another, but they had to go their separate ways.

Universal had great expectations for *Man on the Moon*. Instead of releasing the picture in the spring or summer of 1999, the studio decided to hold it until November. The thinking was that this would position it better for consideration at the end of the year when it came time to give out awards.

The industry was already abuzz over Universal's deal with Carrey for *How the Grinch Stole Christmas*. In September, a bidding war had broken out when Audrey Geisel, widow of Theodore Geisel (who wrote under the name Dr. Seuss) decided to auction rights to the Grinch character. Universal won the contest, in partnership with Ron Howard and Brian Grazer of Imagine Films. One reason for their success was that Mrs. Geisel was a fan of Howard's movies, especially *Apollo 13*.

Directed by Ron Howard, *Grinch* is slated to be released for Christmas 2000. For playing that "nasty wasty skunk" who dresses up as "Santy Claus" and steals presents and trees, Carrey will collect not only $20 million for acting services rendered but also a percentage of revenues from the toys and other merchandise based on the character he plays.

The movie Carrey was supposed to do after *Man on the Moon* hit a snag in the early months of 1999. Cameras were set to roll in Florida on *The Incredible Mr. Limpet*—which was to feature Carrey playing the title role in live action sequences, followed by animation sequences featuring a fish that looked and talked like Jim. But the project fell into limbo when Warner Brothers clashed with Carrey's friend Steve Oedekerk, who was both the writer and director, over the script. In addition, there were technological problems. By March, the movie had been postponed indefinitely, and Carrey was saying he would have to wait and see what he thought of the revised script.

In mid-May Carrey arrived in Rhode Island to begin filming *Me, Myself and Irene*, which reunited him with Peter and Bobby Farrelly, who were writing, directing and producing the picture for Twentieth Century Fox. Since their collaboration with Jim on *Dumb and Dumber* (1994), the Farrelly brothers had scored with the surprise comedy hit of 1998, *There's Something About Mary*.

The Farrelly brothers grew up in Rhode Island, and they set this comedy, and filmed it, on their home turf. As soon as filming began, the town of Jamestown, Rhode Island, found itself in the grip of Carreymania. The filmmakers seemed to be losing control when a mob of kids rushed straight from school to the movie set on a Tuesday afternoon and ignored requests to be quiet.

Carrey plays a Rhode Island state trooper who has developed a split personality disorder. Charlie is a sweet-tempered wimp, but his alter ego, Hank, is a selfish, aggressive bastard. Both Hank and Charlie fall in love with Irene, played by Renee Zellweger, who finds the situation more than a little bewildering. (The plot is more than a little reminiscent of David Cronenberg's *Dead Ringers*, but mercifully played for laughs.)

The docile Charlie will not confront a man in the barbershop who has illegally parked his car for three days, but the explosive Hank decides to commandeer the car and teach the offender a lesson. The most anticipated event for the local community was the filming of a car crashing through the plate-glass window of the barbershop. The scene represents the first time in the movie the audience catches a glimpse of Hank.

All of Jamestown was looking forward to the moment—but by the time it happened, security was so tight that local observers were blocks away. There was a loud bang and a burst of glass when a stuntman drove a yellow Ford Fairlane through the window, but it was all of a bit of an anticlimax.

"I've been in worse car crashes myself," shrugged one disappointed gawker.

A few weeks later, onlookers had forgotten about the crash. Instead they were talking about Jim's romance with Renee Zellweger—prompting memories of his on-set romance five years earlier with another co-star, Lauren Holly.

O O O

IN CREATING the character of Charlie for *Me, Myself and Irene*, Carrey drew on memories of his father, remembering his quiet, good-natured side. Like Stanley Ipkiss, the timid bank clerk in *The Mask*, Percy also had a wild-and-crazy side looking for an excuse to come out. Even after his death, Percy Carrey went on influencing his famous son. Every day Jim was aware of little things he had picked up from Percy—not just his personality and his sense of humor but gestures and the way he carried himself.

Before the release of *Liar, Liar,* Jim had called Rita, alerting her to the fact that she was going to see a playful routine in the film that would have a private meaning for her. And there it was, in the scene where Fletcher scares and delights his son with a beastly, stomach-grabbing thing known as "The Claw." It was a bit of business that Percy had loved doing to his children years earlier, and more recently to his grandchildren.

These were scenes that played over and over in Jim's head, like an old movie you never stop watching—childhood memories, fantasies, dreams of success. The climactic scene, though, was one Jim had scripted himself. After flying home for Percy's funeral in 1994,

Jim had taken the check he had made out to himself—$10 million for services rendered—out of the wallet where he had kept it folded for years. Percy was in his casket when Jim gingerly slipped the check into his father's vest pocket.

It was, in a way, the symbolic gesture that closed the books on family matters. But not even having the wildest fantasy in the world come true—the emergence of Jim Carrey as the world's favorite movie star—could ever really kill the pain. As Jim and Percy both knew, there was only one thing to do: keep on laughing.

fILMOGRAPHY
o o o o o o o

1981: *Introducing Janet* (featured role; made for TV, released on video as *Rubber Face*)
Directors: Glen Salzman and Rebecca Yates

1982: *Copper Mountain* (featured role; made for TV)
Director: David Mitchell

1984: *Finders Keepers* (featured role)
Director: Richard Lester

1985: *Once Bitten* (leading role)
Director: Howard Storm

1986: *Peggy Sue Got Married* (supporting role)
Director: Francis Coppola

1988: *The Dead Pool* (supporting role)
Director: Buddy Van Horn

1989: *The Pink Cadillac* (supporting role)
Director: Buddy Van Horn

1989: *Earth Girls Are Easy* (leading role)
Director: Julien Temple

1991: *High Strung* (cameo)
Director: Roger Nygard

1992: *Doing Time on Maple Drive* (leading role; made for TV)
Director: Ken Olin

1994: *Ace Ventura, Pet Detective* (starring role)
Director: Tom Shadyac

1994: *The Mask* (starring role)
Director: Charles Russell

1994: *Dumb and Dumber* (starring role)
Director: Peter Farrelly

1995: *Batman Forever* (featured role)
Director: Joel Schumacher

1995: *Ace Ventura: When Nature Calls* (starring role)
Director: Steve Oedekerk

1996: *The Cable Guy* (starring role)
Director: Ben Stiller

1997: *Liar, Liar* (starring role)
Director: Tom Shadyac

1998: *The Truman Show* (starring role)
Director: Peter Weir

1998: *Simon Birch* (cameo)
Director: Mark Steven Johnson

1999: *Man on the Moon* (starring role)
Director: Miloš Forman

2000: *Me, Myself and Irene* (starring role)
Director: Peter Farrelly

2000: *How the Grinch Stole Christmas* (starring role)
Director: Ron Howard

Sources

o o o o o o

INTERVIEWS

Joel Axler

Lucy Belvedere
  (Lucy Dervaitis)

Ralph Benmergui

Pat Bradley

Mark Breslin

Bill Brioux

Allan Burns

Malcolm Campbell

Andrew Clark

Suzette Couture

David Creighton

Richard Crouse

John Eindhoven

Joey Gaynor

Eleanor Goldhar

Allan Gould

John Gunn

David Holiff

Larry Horowitz

Bruce Harriott

Pauline Kael

Jack Kapica

John Keyes

Paul King

Dennis Kucherawy

Damien Lee

Ziggy Lorenc

Bob MacAdorey

Mike MacDonald

David Maddison

Danny Marks

Alan Marr

Jamie Masada

Joanne Massey

David Mitchell

Kelly Moran

Buddy Morra

Andy Nulman

Debbie Pearl

Kevin Rooney

Rob Salem

Fred Schreurs

Ron Scribner

Jimmy Shubert

Leatrice Spevack

Michael Steele

David Steinberg

Howard Storm

Jay Tarses

Julien Temple

Fred Tharme

Demi Thompson

Alfred Voytek

Martin Waxman

Rita Zekas

LIBRARIES

In Los Angeles I spent many fruitful days at the amazing Margaret Herrick Library, operated by the Academy of Motion Picture Arts and Sciences. I also made several visits to the Museum of Broadcasting.
In Toronto the library of Cinematheque Ontario provided invaluable resources, as did the Metro Toronto Reference Library at 789 Yonge Street, and the archives of the CBC.

BOOKS

Among the books consulted:

Stand and Deliver, a survey of comedy in Canada by Andrew Clark (published in 1997 by Doubleday Canada Ltd).

Life on Venus Ave., a memoir by Ziggy Lorenc (published in 1997 by Island Nation Press).

Jim Carrey Unmasked, a biography by Roy Traikin (published in 1997 by St. Martin's Press).

VIDEO AND TV

In addition to the movies listed in the filmography, I screened many videos. Among them were *Sam Kinison Live* (1987), the final episode of *The Larry Sanders Show,* and selected episodes of *Later With Bob Costas*, *The Barbara Walters Special*, *Oprah*, *The Tonight Show*, *Late Night With David Letterman, A&E Biography*, and *Celebrity Profile* on E! Channel. And I watched all episodes of *In Living Color* as shown in Canada on the Comedy Network.

INTERNET

On the Internet I found many valuable sources, including the *Jim Carrey Online* website, as well as the archives of *Mr. Showbiz, Entertainment Weekly* and *Variety*.

MAGAZINE ARTICLES

Chatelaine
"Ol' Rubber Face," by Allan Gould, December 1985.

Entertainment Weekly
Ken Tucker's review of *In Living Color*, April 27, 1990.
"Lord Jim," cover story, August 5, 1994.
"King of the Jungle," by Dana Kennedy, November 10, 1995.
Cover story on *The Truman Show*, June 5, 1998.

Details
"Nobody's Fool," by Erik Hedegaard, August 1994.

Esquire
"Renaissance Man," by Martha Sherrill, December 1995.

GQ
"The Wag That Tails the Dog," by John Brodie, August 1994.

Maclean's
"A chameleon comic adapts to success," by Val Ross,
    April 9, 1984.
"The Jim Carrey Show," cover story by Brian D. Johnson,
    June 1, 1998.

Newsweek
"Not Another Pretty Face," July 25, 1994.
"Funny Face," June 26, 1995.

New York:
"The Day the Earth Stood Still for You," by David Denby,
    May 15, 1989.
"Do Not Adjust Your Set," by Chris Smith, June 1, 1998.

The New Yorker
"U.S. Journal: Hollywood, Cal.," January 7, 1980.

Parade
>   "If You Give Up Your Dreams, What's Left?" by Gail
>   Buchalter, January 15, 1995.

People
>   "The Color of Funny," November 11, 1991.
>   "Love With the Proper Co-Star," September 5, 1994.
>   "Doing Just Dandy," June 24, 1996.
>   "Play *Melancholy Baby*," June 9, 1997.
>   "Take Two," June 29, 1998.

Playboy
>   "Jim Carrey's Ride," by Bernard Weinraub,
>   December 1994.

Premiere
>   "Holy Codpiece," May 1995.

Rolling Stone
>   "Jim Carrey: Bare Facts and Shocking Revelations," by Fred
>   Schruers, July 13-27, 1995.
>   A report on VH1 Fashion Awards, December 25, 1997.

Saturday Night
>   "Jim Carrey's Comic Twists," by Shane Peacock, June 1993.

Time
>   "Jim Carrey Breaks Out," June 1, 1998.

Toronto Life
>   "Danny Rose," by Paul King, February 1985.

TV Guide
>   "But Seriously Folks," by Gerald Levitch, September 19, 1981.
>   "On a Roll," by John Keyes, February 18, 1984.
>   "Comedy on the Edge," by Andrew Ryan, March 21, 1992.
>   "*In Living Color*'s Funny Face Plays It Straight," by Bridget
>   Byrne, March 14, 1992.

Vanity Fair
    "The Life of Andy," July 1999.

NEWSPAPERS

Box Office
    "The Man Behind the Mask," by Jon Silberg, August, 1994.

Burlington Post
    "Jim Carrey's Sister Unmasked," by Paul Mitchison,
        March 15, 1998.

Chicago Sun-Times
    "Comedy Zone" column by Ernest Tucker, May 10, 1991.

Hollywood *Drama-Logue*
    "*In Living Color's* Jim Carrey," by Elias Stimac,
        November 14-20, 1991.

Knight-Ridder chain
    "Man of Silly Faces Is Still Open-mouthed,"
        by Frank Bruni, July 3, 1994.

Los Angeles Times
    "They Put Their Best Face Forward," by Chuck Crisafulli,
        July 23, 1994.
    "Unmasking the Masked Maniac," by Michael Walker,
        May 15, 1994.
    "They Bet the Farm—and They Won," by James Bates,
        January 6, 1995.

Newmarket Era
    Interview with Jim Carrey, by Wayne Newton, March 1981.

New York Daily News
    "Carrey's wife is not amused," February 28, 1995.

New York Times
> "Relentlessly Nurturing the Child Within," by Franz Lidz,
> May 3, 1998.

Now (Toronto)
> "Jim Carrey prepares for fame," by Daryl Jung and Shari
> Hollett, April 2, 1982.
> "Carrey Comes Calling," by Rosie Levine, June 11, 1992.

San Francisco Chronicle
> Interview with Jim Carrey, by David Kleinberg,
> March 11, 1990.

Globe and Mail (Toronto)
> "Jim Carrey gets a chance to be himself," by Liam Lacey,
> August 20, 1983.
> "Carrey finds a character of his own," by Laurie Deans,
> April 28, 1984.
> "Carrey's coming up aces," by Cindy Pearlman,
> July 28, 1994.

Toronto Star
> "Up, up goes a new comic star," by Bruce Blackadar,
> February 27, 1981.
> "The Man Who Said No to Johnny Carson," by Rob Salem,
> February 4, 1982.
> "Jim Carrey's Toronto," by Kate Daller, June 16, 1982.
> "Man of 110 faces," by Michael Hanlon, February 27, 1983.
> "Class clown turned class act," by George Gamester,
> October 30, 1984.
> "Carrey credits genetics for his rubber face," by Craig
> MacInnis, July 8, 1994.
> "Jim Carrey: the middle years," by Rob Salem,
> February 14, 1999.

Toronto Sun
> "Will the Real Jim Carrey please stand up?" by Marilyn Linton, August 1981.
> "Even Rodney Dangerfield treats Carrey with respect," by George Anthony, April 1983.
> "Unmasked," by Bruce Kirkland, July 24, 1994.

Variety
> "Fish pic," May 19, 1997.

Village Voice
> "*Earth Girls Are Easy* Wasn't," September 8, 1988.

O   O   O

CHAPTER ONE:

The account of Carrey's debut at Yuk-Yuk's is based on the author's interviews with Joel Axler and Mark Breslin, as well as many published interviews Carrey has given over the years (see above). Material about events of 1999 are drawn from live telecasts of the Golden Globe and Academy Awards presentations.

CHAPTER TWO:

Based on author's interviews with Lucy Dervaitis (Lucy Belvedere), Fred Tharme, Joanne Massey. Other sources: *A&E Biography* and many magazine and newspaper articles, including those in *Parade*, *Maclean's*, *TV Guide*, *Rolling Stone*, the *Toronto Star* and the *Toronto Sun* (as cited above).

CHAPTER THREE:

Account of Percy Carrey's woes is based on author interviews with Pat Bradley, Fred Tharme, Alfred Voytek, John Eindhoven, David

Creighton and Wayne Newton. Additional sources: same as those mentioned in notes for Chapter Two.

CHAPTER FOUR:

Material on Yuk-Yuk's is drawn from author interviews with Mark Breslin, Joel Axler, Ralph Benmergui, Mike MacDonald, Rob Salem, Jack Kapica, Larry Horowitz, Bruce Harriott, Eleanor Goldhar, Suzette Couture.

CHAPTER FIVE:

Based on author's interviews with Leatrice Spevack, Bill Brioux, Demi Thompson, John Gunn, Andrew Clark, Mark Breslin, Joel Axler and Ralph Benmergui. Additional source: Kate Daller's article in the *Toronto Star*, June 16, 1982.

CHAPTER SIX:

Based on author's interviews with Leatrice Spevack, Glen Salzman, Bill Brioux, Dennis Kucherawy and Demi Thompson. Also screenings of private videotapes (from the collections of Leatrice Spevack and Demi Thompson) of Carrey's early performances, and of various appearances by Carrey on the CBC, including *Introducing Janet*. Bruce Blackadar's review of Carrey's act appeared in the *Toronto Star* in February, 1981; Carrey's account of his technique is drawn from Liam Lacey's article in the *Globe and Mail*.

CHAPTER SEVEN:

Based on author's interviews with Demi Thompson, Rob Salem, Leatrice Spevack, Ron Scribner, Damien Lee, David Mitchell, Danny Marks, Ziggy Lorenc, Richard Crouse and David Holiff. Screenings: the movie *Copper Mountain* and the New Year's Eve show from the Imperial Room of Toronto's Royal York Hotel as shown on CBC Television. Rodney Dangerfield's comment was made on *A&E Biography*; Alan Thicke's comment is from E! Channel's *Celebrity Bio*.

CHAPTER EIGHT:

Based on author's interviews with David Holiff, Paul King, Demi Thompson, Ron Scribner, Joey Gaynor, Debbie Pearl. For background, author drew from Calvin Trillin's article in *The New Yorker* and Paul King's article in *Toronto Life*.

CHAPTER NINE:

Based on author interviews with Allan Burns, Jay Tarses, David Holiff, Rita Zekas and Debbie Pearl, as well as screening of *Duck Factory* episodes supplied by Allan Burns and details about the show in Internet files. Other information on the show was drawn from *TV Guide*, Val Ross's article in *Maclean's* and Noel Gallagher's interview with Carrey in the *London Free Press*. Teresa Ganzel's anecdote is from E! Channel's *Celebrity Bio*. Also screened: Carrey's first appearance as a guest on *The Tonight Show*.

CHAPTER TEN:

Author interviews: Allan Burns, David Holiff, Paul King, Debbie Pearl and Lucy Belvedere. Screenings: *Finders Keepers*; Barbara Walters interview with Carrey on ABC pre-Oscar special, March, 1995; episodes of *Duck Factory* as cited above. Print sources: reviews of Carrey's Royal York appearance in 1984 from the *Toronto Star* and the *Toronto Sun*. Review of *Finders Keepers* in *Variety*.

CHAPTER ELEVEN:

Author interviews: Michael Steele, Buddy Morra, David Steinberg, Howard Storm, Fred Schruers and Allan Gould. Screenings: *Rich Little and Friends* (CBC); *Once Bitten*; *Broadway Danny Rose*; *Peggy Sue Got Married*. Reviews of *Once Bitten* in the *New York Times* and

Variety. Information about Carrey and Nicolas Cage is drawn from *A&E Biography*. Anecdote about Las Vegas and Cary Grant is from a 1990 interview with Carrey in the *San Francisco Chronicle*.

CHAPTER TWELVE:

Author interviews: Kelly Moran, Mark Breslin, Joey Gaynor, Jimmy Shubert, Kevin Rooney, Fred Schreurs and Ron Scribner. Articles: *Rolling Stone*, *Newsweek*, *Parade*. Internet files: Sam Kinison. Video: *Sam Kinison Live*, *A&E Biography*, E! Channel *Celebrity Profile*.

CHAPTER THIRTEEN:

Author interviews: Julien Temple, Jamie Masada, Fred Schreurs, Kelly Moran. Screenings: *The Dead Pool*, *Pink Cadillac*, *Earth Girls Are Easy*, *A&E Biography*, *Celebrity Profile*. Articles: *Rolling Stone*, *Now* (1992), Knight-Ridder chain, Hollywood *Drama-Logue* (1991).

CHAPTER FOURTEEN:

Author interviews: Kelly Moran, Mark Breslin, Larry Horowitz, Joel Axler, Andrew Clark, Jimmy Shubert. Screenings: *In Living Color, Later with Bob Costas*. Internet files: *Mr. Showbiz*. Articles: Knight-Ridder chain, *San Francisco Chronicle*, *Saturday Night*, *Entertainment Weekly*.

CHAPTER FIFTEEN:

Author interview: Fred Schreurs. Articles: *San Francisco Chronicle*, *Chicago Sun-Times*, *New York Daily News*, *Los Angeles Times*, *Entertainment Weekly*, *People*, *Saturday Night*, *Rolling Stone*, *GQ*. Screenings: *Ace Ventura, Pet Detective; In Living Color; Later with Bob Costas*.

CHAPTER SIXTEEN:

Author interviews: Jamie Masada, Fred Schreurs, Joel Axler. Screenings: *The Mask, A&E Biography*. Information about song *Heaven Down Here* is from Roy Traikin's *Jim Carrey Unmasked*. Articles: *People, Time, Newsweek, Box Office, GQ, Los Angeles Times, Toronto Star, Toronto Sun*.

CHAPTER SEVENTEEN:

Author interviews: Malcolm Campbell, Fred Schreurs, Pauline Kael. Screenings: *Dumb and Dumber, Batman Forever, Ace Ventura: When Nature Calls, A&E Biography,* ABC interview with Barbara Walters. Articles: *Entertainment Weekly, People, Premiere, Us, Newsweek, Variety, Hollywood Reporter, Rolling Stone, Los Angeles Times, Toronto Star,* Toronto *Globe and Mail,* Hollywood *Drama-Logue*.

CHAPTER EIGHTEEN:

Screening: *The Cable Guy*. Articles: *New York Times, Los Angeles Times, People, Entertainment Weekly, Variety, The Hollywood Reporter, Newsweek*.

CHAPTER NINETEEN:

Author interview: Mike Welsman. Screenings: *Liar, Liar; The Incredible Mr. Limpet*; Jim Carrey interview with Oprah Winfrey, February 1998. Articles: *Burlington Post, People, Entertainment Weekly, Variety, Los Angeles Times*.

CHAPTER TWENTY:

Screenings: *The Truman Show,* episodes of *The Larry Sanders Show, Taxi, Late Night With David Letterman, Saturday Night Live*. Articles: *Time, Maclean's, Entertainment Weekly, People, Vanity Fair, Variety*.

aCKNOWLEDGMENTS

o o o o o o o o o o

tHERE ARE no people more important to a non-fiction writer than sources. I am hugely indebted to many people who trusted me enough to share their memories of Jim Carrey.

Mark Breslin, the founder of Yuk-Yuk's, was almost insanely generous in providing the names and phone numbers of people with valuable insights and good memories. (And it never occurred to him to withhold the names of people who might have old axes to grind against him.) I owe special thanks to Carrey's early managers, Leatrice Spevack, Demi Thompson and David Holiff, and to a former teacher, Lucy Belvedere. Another former teacher, David Creighton, took me on a tour of the Aldershot section of Burlington.

Dianna Symonds and her colleagues at *Saturday Night* came up with an assignment that took me to Los Angeles. Once I was there, Meredith Brody's hospitality gave me the luxury of staying long enough to do a major part of the research on this book. Dan Barton was hugely helpful about helping me make connections. And I was welcomed and helped by, among others, Aviva Whiteson, Ted Kotcheff, Andras Hamori, Vivienne Leebosh, Joan Cohen, Douglas Steinberg and Anne Thompson.

Several people went out of their way to help me track down videos, including Bruce McCulloch, John Gunn, Karen Gruson, Mark Breslin, Roy Harris, Robin Benger, Leatrice Spevack and Kelly Moran.

David McCaughna and Roy Harris helped me find my way to the treasures of the CBC archives. Rosemary Ullyott and Eve Goldin of the library at Cinematheque Ontario answered many questions.

Terry Gillespie and David Hayes brought me out of the dark ages of computer technology. Many videos were provided by Phoenix Movie Rentals.

The team at Penguin Books was supportive in every department, and I am especially indebted to my editor, Meg Masters. Catherine Marjoribanks, our copy editor, made many improvements.

Sara Knelman and Peter Rehak took custom photographs.

Bernadette Sulgit, my partner in all aspects of life, read page proofs and corrected many errors.

Beverley Slopen went far beyond the normal role of a literary agent and did everything possible short of writing the book herself.

O   O   O

iNDEX

o o o o o

224